A Foundation of Ontology

A Foundation of Ontology

A Critical Analysis of Nicolai Hartmann

BY

OTTO SAMUEL

PHILOSOPHICAL LIBRARY
NEW YORK

111
H25
S19

Translated from the German
"Zur Grundlegung der Ontologie. Eine Kritische
Auseinandersetzung mit Nicolai Hartmann."
by Frank Gaynor

PRINTED IN THE UNITED STATES OF AMERICA

WORKS BY NICOLAI HARTMANN

Ethik

Die Philosophie des deutschen Idealismus

Grundzüge einer Metaphysik der Erkenntnis

Das Problem des geistigen Seins

Leibniz als Metaphysiker

Zur Grundlegung der Ontologie

Möglichkeit und Wirklichkeit

Der Aufbau der realen Welt

Die Philosophie der Natur

Teleologische Denken

Aesthetik

CONTENTS

NOTE — Chapters 1, 3, 5, 7 and 9 are the outlines of the teachings of Hartmann. Chapters 2, 4, 6, 8 and 10 contain the critical analysis of his views.

INTRODUCTION

The period between the two World Wars, and the years following the most recent struggle between nations, brought about a truly miraculous achievement in German philosophy — a bright achievement that stands in sharpest contrast to the dark of the political situation in that nation. Husserl's phenomenology produced a new school of philosophic thinking, which uncovered the *apriorism* of phenomena that hitherto had seemed to be accessible solely through the methods of descriptive psychology. Kant's *apriorism* was thus vastly amplified, and investigative efforts, superior in true objectivity to all previously known standards, were concentrated on all intrinsic contents which could be raised before the bracket of what is called "epistemological reduction." Next came Scheler's marvellous investigations of emotional life, producing entirely novel results in the understanding of the sentiments of sympathy and related phenomena, and re-defining morals as a material ethics of values. The young phenomenalist-existentialist movement gained a new leader, of an incredibly high stature, in Martin Heidegger, whose book on Being and Time (*Sein und Zeit*) unveiled prime causes of the Being-Oneself (*Selbstsein*). Jaspers, a Christian existentialist, contributed to the new direction of research by his own analyses.

But they were not the only great personages of German philosophy. We must cite one more man, richly endowed with the productive gift of philosophic thought. His name is Nicolai Hartmann. He was born in Riga in 1882 and died in 1950. He taught in Berlin and in Goettingen. His books attracted wide notice in Germany; they were sold out almost immediately and remained out of print for a long time. First he belonged to the Marburg school of Neo-Kantianism; later, he developed a new ontology based on the teachings of Aristotle and Wolf. His outlook can be termed a sort of Neo-Realism — and yet, this classification is not quite adequate. Nor is there any need for assigning him a place in any set pattern.

Hartmann's life was rich in great accomplishments. He authored seven masterpieces of philosophic literature; three of his earlier writings are still out of print, and my list credits him with twenty-seven other essays and papers. Most probably, though, this is still not the complete record.

I believe that I can render a good service to Americans interested in philosophy by trying to familiarize them with the work of Nicolai Hartmann. In doing so, I would like to pay off a two-fold debt of gratitude — to the German people, for all that for which I am intellectually its debtor, and to my new homeland which received me so charitably when I came to these shores, a persecuted refugee in need of protection and aid.

Hartmann's literary accomplishments in life consist of three parts. The first one comprises the new foundations of ontology. It is composed of three books: *"Zur Grundlegung der Ontologie"* (On the Foundations of Ontology), *"Möglichkeit und Wirklichkeit"* (Possibility and Factuality), and *"Der Aufbau der realen Welt"* (The Structure of the Real World). The last of the three presents the general theory of categories. The second part covers natural philosophy, an introduction to the special theory of categories, furthermore *"Grund- züge einer Metaphysik der Erkenntnis"* (Outlines of a Metaphysics of Knowledge), and *"Das Problem des geis- tigen Seins"* (The Problem of Spiritual Being). The third part is his *"Ethik"* (Ethics).

The present dissertation will be limited primarily to the first of these books, *"Zur Grundlegung der Onto- logie."* This book consists of a thirty-eight-page intro- duction (the reader will find here a condensed, five-page summary) and four individual papers — *"Das Seiende als Seiendes"* (The Extant as Extant), *"Dasein und So- sein"* (Hereness and Suchness), *"Die Realitätsgegeben- heit"* (The Givenness of Reality), and *"Das ideale Sein"* (Ideal Being). Yet, I would be doing an injustice to Hartmann and to my American readers if I were to limit my scope to presenting this one particular book alone. It is my most cherished desire to make this outline of Hartmann's *Grundlegung* the first volume of a series covering the entirety of his work and accomplishments. However, the realization of this intention does not de- pend on me alone; a sufficient degree of public interest is the prime pre-requisite. We must "wait and see."

But I have also a second intention which goes hand in hand with the primary one just mentioned. Much as I have learned from Hartmann, I must confess that there are certain basic points of paramount importance on which I do not agree with him — in fact, to a certain extent, I have reached conclusions quite different from his. This very fact is an evidence of the fruitfulness of the reading of philosophical texts, too. One learns not a philosophy, but the art of philosophizing, which pos- sesses a freedom of its own. This is why I cannot confine myself to merely quoting, without criticism, the intrinsic substance of Hartmann's teachings; I have considered it my duty to state clearly in what I differ with him. And this is entirely a matter of objective reasons. But I shall consistently proceed so as to permit the reader to obtain an entirely objective picture of Hartmann's teachings before I present my criticism, in separate sections. If a reader wishes merely to gain insight into Hartmann's world of thought, he need not give more than a cursory glance to the sections where I present my own views. Yet, I hope that the reader will take an interest also in getting acquainted with a certain opposing trend of thought, which, to a certain extent at least, can be named Neo-Realism. I would feel amply rewarded if this could make the reader's understanding of Nicolai Hartmann all the more fruitful, whether he will choose to agree with the proffered criticism or to reject it.

The American reader might welcome the remark that Nicolai Hartmann must not be confused with Eduard von Hartmann, another great philosopher (1842-1906). The latter acquired fame through his philosophy of the Unconscious, but later he published more valuable papers, especially on the problem of categories, in which Nicolai Hartmann, too, was keenly interested. Max Scheler holds Eduard von Hartmann in very high esteem, and he analyzes his ideas critically — although just occasionally.

As for the sections of criticism (the even-numbered ones — Sections 2, 4, 6, etc.) I might be accused of emulating Penelope of the classical myth who would weave a cloth by day, under coercion by her suitors, merely to unravel its threads at night. But this would apply to me to a certain extent only. Hartmann's conclusions possess substantial solidity. I am happy to recognize his merits and to state that I have learned a great deal from him. I am profoundly convinced that Being *(Sein)* is an a priori unit, to be comprehended both transcendent-realistically and transcendental-idealistically. This is no speculative prejudgment, in the sense of a prejudice, but the *result* of many years of research and thinking. To be sure, I am bound to differ with Hartmann as regards his failure to do full justice to the transcendental-idealistic moment in pure Being, and in this respect I may seem, more or less, to be emulating Penelope. But Hartmann is a first-rate transcendent-realist, and as for his handling here the genuine moments of the interpretation of Being, I stand to Hartmann as Penelope to Odysseus, her true husband whom she loved and revered. The sections reflecting my own critical judgment are to be construed in this two-fold sense.

And now a word about my summaries. Faithful accuracy was my principal concern here. A modest service, this — yet one that imposes a certain responsibility. The main point was to find the proper balance in my condensation, to make it neither too long nor too short. I believe to have succeeded in this. Thus, for instance, I have condensed the thirty-eight-page introduction to five typewritten pages. The first treatise, comprising forty-eight pages, is summed up in twelve pages of typescript. I believe that this is just the right proportion. It will give the American reader a true insight into Hartmann's world of ideas. Of course, the perusal of digests can never fully take place of a study of the German original. Let us hope that Hartmann's writings will be translated into English some day.

My second consideration was to produce a truly readable text. As a rule, I use Hartmann's own words, especially his technical terms. This is no more than logical and obvious. But on the other hand, I did not make myself a slave to this rule. I would frequently feel free to deviate from it. Wherever a concise term seemed to be helpful in improving on the text, I would use it, even though it had not been employed by Hartmann. In a few instances, I even anticipated a little and threw in a comment which does not appear at that particular spot in Hartmann's own writing but belongs to another part of it. However, I did so but very rarely. For instance, where Hartmann speaks of form and matter, I stated that this was our first step into a "Hall of Fame." You will not find this expression in Hartmann's text. This is one of the few instances where I substituted a plastic expression of my own for Hartmann's copiousness of style which I was unable to follow, in order to present a text of practical use to the American reader.

Thus, I submit my friendly debate with Nicolai Hartmann to the American public. Every philosophical conclusion is the fruit of a monologue in conjunction with discussions with others. This is what constitutes its dialectic nature. I would like to extend this discussion. I do not ask the American reader, "Which of the two of us is right — Hartmann or myself?" — for neither of us has any claim on the absolute truth. But I do ask the reader, "Who is *more* right?" I would be very happy if a great many of my readers would let me know their verdicts. Those who care to do so, kindly write to me in care of the publishers.

Finally, the reader may want to know whether any good books outlining the doctrines of Hartmann have ever been published in the English language. The answer is, *No.* Hartmann's *Ethik* itself has been published in an English translation, but as to books suitable for introducing the American reader to Hartmann's philosophy, I have been able to discover just one single such publication, a book entitled *"Personality. A Study according to the Philosophies of Value and Spirit of Max Scheler and Nicolai Hartmann," by* Eckhard Joseph Koehle (Newton, N. J., 1941; Thesis, Columbia University, 1941). I immediately communicated with Mr. Koehle, and I found that his doctoral dissertation was already out of print and could not be obtained in book stores. The reader can get to see this book in some library which has a copy of it on file — for instance, the New York Public Library. This circumstance is another evidence of the fact that there is a real need for a guide book to introduce the American reader to this philosophy, and that the American public will welcome it with acute interest.

I wish to express sincere thanks and appreciation to Mr. Frank Gaynor for his fine English translation of my German manuscript, and for the care and interest which he has taken in this work.

O. S.

1

WHY MUST WE RETURN TO ONTOLOGY?

In the introductory passages of his *"Zur Grundle-gung der Ontologie,"* Hartmann poses the question, *"Why must we return to ontology?"* The Introduction of his book, pp. 1-38, is devoted to answering this question. The question of Being *(Sein)* concerns the Extant *(das Seiende)* — that-which-is — as such. The old ontology was followed by idealistic and relativistic modes of explanation which questioned the role of cognitional knowledge as the true comprehension of an Extant *per se (Ansichseiendes)*. Natural-scientific relativism endeavored to convert the substrata of density, pressure, work, weight, space, time, matter and movement into mere relationships. Biology is the second field which presents metaphysical residual problems. Life is a situation given for us in two parallel ways — externally and internally. It is something else to the physician than it is to the patient in the direct consciousness of his self. This leads to a causalistic view and to a teleological view, both of which might make the mistake of missing the true determinative element in life, which constitutes the metaphysical problem of biology.

The next field is that of psychic life. The metaphysical element is missed here if the act is confused with the experiencing of the act. If so, psychologism is the result. Psychic life is unbound by space, and yet no less real than the physical world.

Hartmann borrows from Hegel the concept of the objective spirit, the non-personal spirit, which has to do with justice, morality, *ethics,* art, religion and science. Its mode of being *(Seinsweise),* too, requires thorough investigation — feasible ontologically only. The metaphysical residual problems encountered here can be only tackled today through a preliminary effort. Objective spirit is neither consciousness nor subject — and this is the key to the secret of its special mode of being.

The sphere of logic, too, has its metaphysics. True and false judgments float about in the sphere of history, but the power of judgment possesses neither temporality nor reality, but an irreality which is a kind of ideality. And conclusions are valid, even where they are not carried out. Is a co-existence of contradictions impossible in the real world, too? And how is this logical transference to the Real possible? Laws of logic must be expected to be universal laws of Being, too.

A regrettable fact is the decadence of the problem of knowledge. Kant saw the truth when he said that the categories of experience are at the same time categories of the objects of experience. But his own transcendental idealism did not remain at the lofty heights of this insight. This is why psychologism and logism invaded epistemology, and logism equated cognition and judgment. Thus, various thinkers — such as Natorp, Cassirer, Rickert, Husserl, Heidegger — fell for the error of the correlativistic argument that no object could be without subject. It is a late descendant of the *intellectus infinitus et divinus*. This makes knowledge cease to be the comprehension of something extant *per se*. The world is then extant only insofar as it becomes known. The difference between True and Untrue goes by the board, for the inner agreement of knowledge with itself is not sufficient to constitute it. The possibility of the existence of fantasy, thinking, erroneous judgment, can then no longer be explained. The contrast between genuine comprehension and mere ideation, thinking, opinion, judgment, is razed in that case.

But the truth is that the Extant *(das Seiende)* — our *that-which-is* — becomes an object by objectivation. Not every Extant necessarily becomes an object. The two concepts must not be confused. We recognize an Extant only if and as it has been objectified. The Extant has a supramaterial existence. We do not create the material object. The epistemological relation is not resolved into the subject-object correlativity. It builds on an image of the material object. The Extant *per se* is that which is recognized — not a mere appearance. This was Kant's error. "I recognize something" is equivalent to "something appears to me," but this is a tautological proposition. But that which appears in the appearance is the Extant *per se*. Without it, the appearance would be a mere make-believe, more difficult to explain for knowledge than the appearing Extant *per se*. The character of Being is an exclusive property of material objects. Epistemology tends to transform itself into Theory of Being. For also the subject is an Extant, and thus the epistemological relationship is a relationship of Being at the same time.

The realm of knowledge is not the last one to harbor metaphysical residual problems. So do the realms of Ethos and Freedom. Man stands in the midst of the current of happenings as the one affected by it. Here we encounter genuine teleology. In the state of being compelled to make a decision, man is free. Thus, the phenomena of reckoning, justification, guilt and merit, make their appearance. Only he who is capable of evil can also be good and do good. The self-determination of man does not refer merely to the antinomy of causality, but also to the antinomy of the Ought. This is the seat of the metaphysicality of ethics, which must be served by a value-theory.

The situation with respect to this metaphysics of values is this: The fountain-head of the Ought is not practical reason, as Kant saw it. This leads to the paradoxon that man would have to obey or violate a self-given law. But what is the mode of Being of the Ought and of values? The understanding of moral autonomy hinges on the answer to this question. A value is something ideal, and yet not like a mathematical principle which has a binding force like a natural law. It is comprehended through a feeling of values. Is the value absolute or relative? Is this a repetition of the query for the relationship between perceptor and Extant? New tasks are laid before the analyst here.

We encounter metaphysical elements, furthermore, in art and beauty. The artist enchants us through a magic of appearance. Two totally different modes of being are linked into one unit. The canvas, the frame, the spots of pigment in a painting hanging on the wall, are parts of a real mode of Being. But the painting has it own space, its own perspective, its own landscape. The irreal-ideal mode of Being is embedded in the real one, and the two together form an inseparable unit. This is how the artist enchants us through the magic of appearance. A new ontological problem is encountered here.

The last field in which we encounter metaphysical

residual problems is that of history. Their mode of Being is that of the objective spirit in its relationship to the individuals as the vehicles. Does accidentality or necessity obtain here? Do we behold here the ghastly countenance of the senseless, or may we dare speak of a fulfillment of sense? Are we to interpret the historical process causalistically or finalistically? Or does it show still another, quite different form of determination? Which is right — the economic theory or the doctrine of the spirit — Marx or Hegel? Is the historical process to be comprehended from above or from below? Perhaps both Marx and Hegel are wrong, for causality and finality run contrary to each other, and both prove inadequate. But then what? What other type of determination can we introduce?

These metaphysical problems are scattered far and wide over the various fields, and yet form a close framework. They are irrational, but not totally so. That which is ontological in them — the modes of Being, the types of determination, the structural laws, the categorical forms — happens to be just what is relatively the most non-metaphysical in this metaphysics, and for this very reason, the easiest to manage. This is why the hope of a limited understanding comes to new life here. It is the thought of a new *philosophia prima*. It is the doctrine of the Extant as Extant. But basically, this *philosophia prima* is a *philosophia ultima*. For the *ratio essendi* and the *ratio cognoscendi* run diametrically opposed to each other. We must start out from that which is ontologically secondary. And just as the way of knowledge has this prime freedom as against the order of Being, the way of representation lays claim to a second freedom as against the way of knowledge.

And so we may well re-adopt a great many of the

points dealt with by the old ontology: *de notione entis, de essentia et existentia, de singulari et universali, de possibili et impossibili, de necessario et contingente, de determinato et indeterminato, de principio rationis sufficientis, de principiis, de ordine rerum, de dependentia, de simplici et composito.*

A PHILOSOPHY OF ONTOLOGY

2

THE INCOMPLETE APPROACH OF HARTMANN

Our criticism will start on Hartmann's statement about the nature of knowledge *(Erkenntnis)* — that it is the true comprehension, recognition of an Extant *per se;* that we recognize an Extant only insofar as it has been objectified; that the Extant has a superobjective Being. With the one-sidedness of these assertions, Hartmann seems to have wholeheartedly embraced transcendent realism. His statement is not wrong, but it only tells half of the story. If his idealistic opponents, such as Kant (for in this respect Hartmann is an opponent of Kant), Rickert, the Neo-Kantians, Husserl, and Heidegger, start a transcendentalization of this transcendent realism, they *are* partly right — that which does not yet mean that transcendentalization in one form or another is the whole truth which must be set against the views of Hartmann, Hartmann can still be right in many a point, and furthermore, the transcendentalization itself must have a continuation in Truth, perhaps with drastic changes into something totally different.

But what is meant here by "transcendentalization"? Its basic definition may be "a correlation of object and subject," but this phrase is certainly still very deficient, for the very reason that the subject, itself, is also an Extant. In order to explain the cognition of the Extant, it may be found necessary to bring in something subject-like, and in the course of further investigation this sub-ject-like something may turn out after all to be some-thing entirely else than a subject, also to be no subject at all, or to be a transcendental subject. But all this may lead nearer to the truth, and in that case, the work of Kant, of the Neo-Kantians, of the phenomenalists and of the existentialists would not seem to have been futile as Hartmann believes. It might even be possible that cognition is fully transcendent-realistic, a genuine per-ception of an Extant *per se,* and wholly transcendental-idealistic at the same time, a productive demonstration of the material object. To be sure, this would mean a relationship dialectical through and through, totally inexpressible in terms of formal logic without contradic-tion — but can we expect anything else when touching on the ultimate things of cognition? In this sense, it may be true that Hartmann was right but told just half the story; in other words, that he makes himself be wrong by simply failing to see the other, the idealistic, side of the cognition. From the dialectical "wholly-wholly" he deletes the second "wholly," and thereby he changes the whole of cognition into a flatly transcendent-realistic relationship, and he misses entirely the immeasurable depth, beauty and fecundity of transcendental idealism. The logical consequence is that his philosophical thought, rich as it is, remains nevertheless close to the merely natural-scientific pattern of thinking. However, since it is so complete and fertile in its fashion, a critical debate is the very thing to highlight its other, idealistic, side all the better and all the more fully. This is what makes a discussion with him so fruitful.

Kant already tried to combine realism and idealism

in this manner. Yet, he did not do it so sweepingly dialectically as it is proposed here. He stated that his criticism as a preparation for a future metaphysics was empirical realism and transcendental idealism at the same time, and this is the sense in which the phrase underlined by Hartmann, stating that the categories of experience are at the same time the categories of the objects of the experience, holds true. Let us not go into any more details here; let it be said merely that we go Kant's combination of realism and idealism one better by saying that true ontology is transcendent realism and transcendental idealism at the same time.

But we must proceed with great care here. Let us therefore assign the symbol for "unknown" to the idealistic countermoment, which is omitted by Hartmann, the subject-like something which as an Extant must be included in the scheme of an explanation of cognition. Let us call it X. The mathematician proceeds this way when trying to ascertain the value of the unknown quantity in an equation found to be a rational one. But our case is something quite different, and our procedure is absolutely no emulation of the mathematical method. That just will not suit philosophy.

This X can be many things: subject, a subject-like something, a transcendental subject, an intermediate stage, a limit, a third neutral factor, an extant contradiction, an existential impossibility, existence itself not as *What* but as positing of the *That*, the already mentioned dialectic *wholly-wholly*. Its limit character could be determined in the most various manners — as a borderline between the total otherness of a Being-like-Non-Being and an abundance, as a borderline between Being and Extant. The extant contradiction contained in it could be investigated with a view to ascertaining its structure. The Hegelian principle of the spirit, the being once again totally the Self in the Other of itself, and thus the return into itself, could be a special case of this structure of Being. This X could be interpreted also as an assimilation of the Extant to its Being, of the existing to existence in general, and thus, to a certain extent, as the "*is*-dimensionality" (*Istförmigkeit*) of the Extant. This is how the irrational would undergo a transcendentalization, which would remain inaccessible to every transcendent realism. In fact, this X might turn out to be also that which is really meant by the word *God*. Thus, the affinity would be the explanation also of every transcendental idealism by religion, and also of that aversion showed by Hartmann to the religious world of phenomena, which we will discuss later.

This X is perhaps something of all this, and yet it might be that the true essence of this transcendental X could not at all be grasped this way either. For this reason, it is good to apply a most general formula to this transcendental, calling it simply X. At any rate, we notice that we are dealing with something missed by Hartmann, but which we need in order to explain cognition as well as the Extant as an Extant — in other words, to be able to epistemologize as well as to ontologize. But we need this countermoment in order to rid transcendent realism of the death which gains a foothold in it if the cognitive transcendent view of the Extant *per se* is to remain the last word which then makes epistemology and ontology a quasi-natural science. Against this mortal danger, we need the transcendentalization of the transcendent, the first stages of the recognition of which were opened up by Kant. This precious heritage must not be squandered. We have here no free choice, such as — let us say — that of expediency; the very problems themselves drive us toward this countermoment — the very problems which we endeavor to serve in objective faithfulness.

Hartmann is undoubtedly right in holding that some Extant *per se* appears in the appearance, and that without this, the phenomenon would be reduced to mere semblance. This is true insofar as transcendent realism speaks up. At the same time, however, it holds true that the Extant *per se,* which remains ever unknowable to transcendent realism, poses a question for transcendental idealism, a question to be elaborated, and it introduces an ever farther-going, deeper-reaching cognitive process which then benefits that very transcendent realism, too.

The decay into psychologism and logism occurs if transcendent realism cannot assert itself in the face of trancendental idealism. In this, Hartmann is right. But the failings and partialities of transcendentalism have nothing to do with its truth and validity, and X is to be defined more thoroughly, transcendental idealism may vanish — as a *name,* but not as a *concept.* We must not forget that we are dealing with the youngest of all researches on cognition, which still has not gotten over its growing pains. Cognition and judgment must certainly not be called identical. The *intellectus infinitus et divinus* must not shunt the exploration of X to a dead-end track. But all these shortcomings can be overcome. The new whole, in which trancendent realism and transcendental idealism are combined, is capable of divorcing truth and error still better and more safely than can transcendent realism alone, which after all rests on hypostatization and false absolutization.

The appearance is an out-and-out image in yet quite another sense than can be comprehended by transcendent realism, the imagery of which is secondary in comparison with it. And at the same time, in the transcendental-idealistic sense, the phenomenon possesses the full inflexibility of the reality which transcendent realism ascribes to the Extant *per se*. And because transcendent realism does not make a clear distinction between the two, it lapses again into the old mistake, denounced by Kant, of confusing the thing-in-itself (*Ding an sich*) and appearance, and treating the appearance as a thing-in-itself. However, it still holds true, at that, that every idealistic elimination of the thing-in-itself fails.

Exactly insofar as the subject is also an Extant, and the cognitive relationship is a relationship of Being, and the laws of logic are laws of Being (all of this is granted by Hartmann), the transcendental heads into the transcendent realism, to its own benefit. This is why Hartmann could not avoid making the innumerable findings which bear the mark of idealism. We can cite here the twofold givenness of life (physician and patient), the non-spatial reality of the psychic, the mode of Being of the objective spirit, the timelessness of the sense of judgment, the metaphysics of *ethos* and of freedom, the ideal Being of values, individual self-determination, the mode of Being of the Ought, the metaphysics of art and of beauty as a union of two modes of being, his great historical-metaphysical query. Hartmann is no realist in the sense of Bentham or Reid. He has nothing to do with the superficial reality of "sound" human reason, although he has full understanding for this phenomenon, too, and he gives it a positive evaluation. Also, the idealistic elements in his realism go much farther than with the American neo-realists and critical realists. Hartmann, himself, is a critical realist, in the best sense of the term, one who possesses the most profound knowledge also of transcendental idealism of every coinage and takes over from it whatever is possible. He is a leader in his time and a master of philosophic thought. This brief introduction is still inadequate to permit a full appraisal. This is something that is still to unfold. But all these idealistic elements within his transcendent realism, which appear to make him free of any preconceived attitude, and which are instrumental to an ontology bent upon understanding the Extant as such, are still patterned on the cognition of an Extant *per se* (*Ansichseiendes*). This confines his idealism. He coordinates himself with the basic scheme of transcendent realism and subordinates himself to it. This is what remains the decisive factor. Thus, for instance, a number, recognized as an ideal entity, plays fully the part of a quasi-thing-in-itself, with all the concreteness of a material object. Now then, this is by no means wrong, but it is one-sided. From the idealistic viewpoint, there is something else still to be considered — and this is just what Hartmann fails to do. He sees the natural-scientific basic type of the cognition of the *per se* extending into the highest fields. Insofar as Hartmann grants that certain aspects of transcendentalization are weakened by the adherence to this trancendent-realistic type, he ceases to be a critical realist. He becomes uncritical. Mistakes become apparent and call for refutation and correction. He remains trapped within this boundary, for he believes that this is the only way for him to get along with a minimum of the metaphysical, and because speculative pre-judgments and prejudices contradict the vigorous sense of responsibility of his philosophical conscience. This is praiseworthy, indeed. But the decisive problem is not to get along with a minimum of metaphysics, but to recognize and apply the right dose of metaphysics which will do justice to the factual situation of the problems, be that a maximum or a minimum or a medium dose. Hartmann, unfortunately, failed to recognize this. His just fear of undisciplined, free and wild speculation, against which the Critique of Pure Reason is a sole mighty warning, misguided him into settling in a minimum of the metaphysical, without inquiring whether this does not ravish the problems. This is why he did not become quite so free from the preconceived attitude as he believed himself to be. His transcendent realism bears a basic pattern which is purely dogmatic, in the strongest sense of the word. But within the framework of this truly human limitation, he displays a greatness which puts him in the rank of the foremost thinkers.

Thus, we take up the call of Nicolai Hartmann: "Back to Ontology!" — but not because the ontological is the relatively most non-metaphysical element in metaphysics, and therefore the easiest to handle, but because its very union of the transcendent-realistic and transcendental-idealistic makes it represent the intrinsic riches of the metaphysical in metaphysics, that wealth which, in squandering itself on the cognition, summons not to the easiest but the most objectively factual treatment.

3

ON THE EXTANT AS EXTANT IN GENERAL

The first one of the four treatises included in the *Grundlegung* is entitled *"Vom Seienden als Seienden überhaupt"* (On the Extant as Extant at all). It comprises three sections, consisting of ten chapters. The following is a summary of its contents.

Section I — The Concept of the Extant and its Aporia.
Chapter I — The Fundamental Question of Ontology.

A departure can be made from this side of realism and idealism. It only seems to be different because of the habit of understanding Being *(Sein)* as Being *per se (Ansichsein)*. But the phenomenon must be viewed first without interpretation. One must not form any arbitrarily speculative prejudgment. He who tries to do so, is not yet on realistic grounds.

A careful distinction must be made between Being *(Sein)* and the Extant, that-which-is *(Seiendes)*. The interrelationship of the two is the same as that of Truth and the True, of Reality and the Real, of Factuality and the Factual — of *esse* and *ens*. Unfortunately, these pairs of concepts have always been confused with each other. Being *(Sein)* is the *One* the identical in the manifoldness of the Extant. Naturally, the two must not be separated from each other, but the lack of distinction has led to viewing Being as a substance.

The Aristotelian version of the question is helpful today still. Its chosen task is to explain Being as Extant, or the Extant as such. This clearly points up Being as such as something general, although the wording uses the term "Extant." Aristotle, too, failed to overcome the peril of substantialism, but the latter can be avoided by adhering faithfully to his wording. It is a wonderful formula. Just how wonderful it is can best be recognized by seeing how much it wards off. If Being is regarded as appearance or as something in the state of becoming, the formula is violated. Such a cognition does not involve a cognition of the Extant as Extant. Likewise in the case of the Extant as something posited, meant, imagined and subject-referred. For Being is not absorbed in the objecthood (Gegenstandsein). This is the supreme meaning of the Aristotelian formula which hits well the formal meaning of the fundamental question. Heidegger tried in vain to defend himself against it.

Chapter 2:

It is worth our while to take a closer look at Heidegger's abortive attempt. He abandoned Aristotle's formula for the other one which queries for the sense and meaning of Being. Heidegger's concept of hereness (Dasein) remains completely man-bound. Hereness (Dasein) is Being (Sein) that understands its own Being*. This is why the Extant (Seiendes), the world, Truth, are the ever-mine. This prejudges everything, and such an

* It is Being concerned by its own Being, and which thus is Being-in-the-World. — O.S.

16

analysis of Being ends up as the analysis of givenness. The modes of givenness are the modalities of Being. The objective spirit is de-powered, the stratum of Being (*Seinsschicht*) of the historical spirit become impalpable. The personal decision of the individual alone is proven right.

It is wrong to twist the question of Being into a question of meaning. It is as proper to inquire about the Being of meaning as about the Meaning of Being. Yet, this is not the general question of Being. Meaning exists always only for somebody. There is no meaning-in-itself. The Being of the Extant stands indifferent to whatever the Extant might be "for somebody."

Chapter 3 — The Attitude of Ontological Cognition.

Being *(Sein)* is the ultimate and therefore cannot be defined. It is impalpable, the out-and-out universal. It cannot even be delimited against something else, such as some other universal. Only the contentual element of a mode of Being can be indicated, not the mode of Being itself.

But this irrationality is merely partial. Therefore, it cannot be defined and cannot be typed by characteristics, but the way from the general to the special is open, and this circumstance makes it necessary to bring in certain specific questions. This is the path which we take in this treatise.

There is a circumstance which proves useful in this reflection on the aporia of generality and indeterminacy of the Extant as Extant, of the Extant as such, of Being at all — ontology is a re-approach to the natural. This makes one ponder the difference between natural and reflected attitude. Cognition is directed at its object, at that which it perceives, and not at that which constitutes the cognition. If we want to reach some conclusion on it, we must go into the attitude called reflection, which is a bending-back *(re-flexion)*, whereas cognition stands for the natural. This bending-back becomes a source of aporias in epistemology. The same thing occurs in psychology. Acts are not given, like objects. The hardest task in this respect is that of logic, if it wants to make its object not the contentual element of the concepts, but the concepts themselves. This is why it has so often slipped from its own plane onto those of psychology, epistemology or ontology. We have thus found three fields in which the natural attitude must be replaced be a reflected one, involving diverse complications.

Borrowing certain concepts from scholasticism, from Wilhelm von Occam in particular, let us call the natural attitude *intentio recta,* and the reflected bending-back *intentio obliqua.* Then we can say that ontology is the restoration of the *intentio recta.*

Chapter 4 — Position and Roots of the Problem of Being.

Three principal fields are present in the *intentio recta*: the natural, the scientific, and the ontological relationships to the world. Moreover, however, we classify epistemology, psychology and logic under the heading "Philosophy," not under "Science." Ontology continues the natural trend which starts in the pre-scientific, and which is taken over by natural science and also by the science of the mind. The recognition of the right, for instance, represents an unreflected mental attitude, and the same holds true for the other fields of objective spirit, in strong contradistinction to epistemology, psychology and logic. Ontology is, therefore, in this respect, a continuation. In the case of the *intentio recta* of natural science, the external material form of the givenness *(Gegebenheit)* is still predominant. Thus, all these fields, in contradistinction to the other three, show a common relationship to the Extant, the essential trend of a natural realism which knows that taking something for an object is not the same as taking something for an Extant.

As contrasted with the naive world-awareness, however, enormous contentual differences are involved here, but the unity of the object range remains intact in the four fields. The object is the same, but the view of the object changes. Something of the prescientific naive view is preserved in the theory. The word *theory* means *view*.

The *intentio obliqua* misses the given aspect of the Extant. Reflection gets always only as far as the objects and does not reach the Extant. It is therefore all too likely to wander into the blind alley of the immanence of the awareness. Thus, gnosiology wants to hold fast *in* the reflectedness of the awareness of it. Without gaining a firm footing ontologically, gnosiology here misses it own object — cognition.

Phenomenology does not get as far as the things (as it so strongly emphasizes), but merely as far as the phenomenon of the thing. It becomes tuned to things through *intentio recta* — to the phenomena by *intentio obliqua*. That which is given is grasped mentally in the reflected attitude. This casts a light on what the phenomenological methods calls "bracketing" *(Einklammerung)*, "reduction" *(Reduktion)*, and raising before the bracket" *(Vor-die-Klammer-Heben)*.

Section II — Traditional Views on the Extant (Sei-endes)

Chapter 5 — Naive and Substantial Concept of Being.

The Extant is first grasped mentally as a Thing *(Ding)*. Then, as something given in a world in which it comes into being and passes into nothingness again. The front of Being *(Seinsfront)* falls back here already. Now then, either the Extant is what is evidenced by the senses — and this leads to Berkeley's *esse est percipi* — or the Extant is that which is now, the present, and in that case, whatever is past or future is non-existent. This is how Parmenides described Being as the Eternal Now. Then comes the νοειν. Senses and the present are no longer sufficient. Past and future invade Being meaningfully.

This, then, leads to the other extreme. Only that which is hidden, inner, non-given, is the Extant proper, that which truly exists. But why? There is no slightest reason for such a distinction of the Extant *as Extant*. Next comes the development of doctrines of a world basis, of the prime substance, of the elements, of the Idea, of the Substance, of the thing-in-itself *(Ding-an-sich)*. Distinction is made between the real world and an apparent one. But this is no difference as to Being! The Extant is completely indifferent to it.

In the ideas of antiquity on substance, we see three ontological main motives: 1) The substance is that which is independent, that which gives support. But that which is supported is also extant. The law of indifference obtains again. — 2) Monistic tendencies to unity. But plurality is no less extant. Again the law of the indifference of the Extant obtains, revealing the tendencies to unity as a rationalistic prejudice. — 3) **Perpetuality**, in antithesis to Becoming. But the same thing must be stated once again. In the world, something will never issue forth out of nothing, but always out of something. The same holds true for passing away. Things change into each other. On the other hand, if the nothing is introduced doubly into the definition of Becoming, an inferiority complex will develop with respect to it, whereas Becoming is no less real and existing than the perpetual. Heraclitus already corrected this error. Only the perpetual can be capable of changing.

Furthermore, the Extant is viewed as a substratum and as a definite, as matter and form, and this is where we enter a hall of fame. Substratal thoughts become the doctrine of the indeterminate, the *apeiron*. In contrast, the throne of Being is won by the definite, the definition, the boundary (in conformity with the Greek spirit), the shape of ideas, the form possessing proportion and beauty. This makes Being seem to gain perfectness of unambiguity, affirmation, comprehensibility, and conceivability. The worlds of ideas of Plato and Aristotle open up. The more determinatives a thing has, the more real it is. Matter is alogical. Yet, both are not the Extant as Extant, but merely some secondary property of it.

The equation of *ens* and *bonum* makes its appearance. Form = Being, and Form = Value, therefore Being = Value. And the higher is the Form, the higher are Being and Value. We are here in the midst of Aristotle's teleology. This is metaphysical optimism. The imperfect, the worthless and evil are equally extant and factual. They cannot be explained as semblance and as non-existent. Being as such knows no grades.

Chapter 6 — *The Extant* (Seiendes) *as Universal and Singular*

Being *(Sein)* becomes *Wesenheit, essentia.* Many previous motives, such as reason, unity, the perpetual, definiteness, form value principle, the intrinsic, the *telos* of Becoming, have a share in the formation of this concept of Being and lead through Aristotle to the medieval battle over the universals. The individual case is pushed into the background. Ideal Being, without temporality, past, motion, change, delights the eyes of the onlooker by a perfection. But, unfortunately, it also lacks existence, concreteness and vital spark. It was a good thing to recognize the Being of the general, for it is by no means self-evident. Only the essentialities *(Wesenheiten)* are the Being proper. But if that *of which* they are essentialities is null and non-existent, are they, themselves, not nonexistent essentialities? This is what made the communicatory theories of scholasticism the most successful.

But now the individualization with which Aristotle could no longer cope attracts the look of a counter-movement. Individuals differ psychologically and intellectually, and so the attempt is made to individuate the *eidos.* Plotinus postulates essential forms *(Wesensformen)* of the Individual. But this means a sacrifice of the difference between essential and accidental determinations. Duns Scotus regards form as the *principium individuationis.* Quiddity is composed of the same determinants of essentialities *(Wesenheiten).* Individuality is haecceitas differentiated to the utmost degree. Leibniz knows ideas of individual things. But this way of thinking leads to a dilemma: Either is individuality based on matter, and thus on a non-essential, or the *essentia* ceases to be universal. The fault lies in the one-sided concept of Being. The principle of the Extant as Extant is violated.

A hopeful glance is now directed at the *existentia,* as opposed to the *essentia.* The Extant *(Seiendes)* is that which exists *(Existierendes).* This invites the appearance of nominalism. The universal becomes almost devoid of essence. It has no Being, it is only there *in mente.* Suchness *(Sosein)* and hereness *(Dasein)* come face to face with each other. The occurrence of individual cases, about which the *essentia* means nothing, is *existence (Existenz).* Yet, the shaping, specifically, is a matter of the *essentia.* Does nominalism not commit here the same mistake of isolation as the realism of the universalia? The Extant *(Seiendes)* as such can only be a union of *essentia* and *existentia.*

Chapter 7 — The Extant (Seiendes) *as a Structural Element and as a Whole*

The antithesis of individuality and generality *(Allgemeinheit)* must be distinguished carefully from that of the individual and the all-ness *(Allheit).* In summary, we may say: "Pure individuality in itself exists no more than does pure generality in itself. Everything that exists is individual (and vice versa), and every definiteness is, formally, a generality. But the general is real only *in* the individual feature, for only the latter has existence; and the individual feature has definiteness only in what it has in common with something else, *i.e.,* in that which is formally general in it." (Pp. 66-67.) The first antithesis is qualitative, the second one is quantitative. Every all-ness *(Allheit)* is an individual feature which has individuality.

The Extant as an individual, element and member, leads to atomistic thinking. The word "individual" is merely a translation of the word *atom.* Thus, a theory of sensations was formulated. This includes the immaterial substantiality of the monads of Leibniz. In Sociology, the atomistic thinking denies the true reality of family, nation and state. But this entire school of thought falls with its sensualistic premise. The Extant as Extant is no part, no element, no individual. The part exists solely for the whole. There are no grades of Being *(Sein),* Reality *(Realität)* and Existence *(Existenz),* only grades of their order of magnitude, sharpness of form and distinctness.

The other side in the argument takes the Extant as all-ness, wholeness and system. Hegel said: Truth is the Whole. There are no independent elementary configurations. They derive their distinctness of Being from the higher whole. The seizure of a fortress is an element of a political plan. The cells within the organism preach this same truth of the whole. But here, too, Being is confused with a specific category of Being. A particle of dust is no less extant than the universe.

Section III — Definitions of the Extant (Seiendes) *from the Mode of Being* (Seienweise).

Chapter 8 — *Factuality* (Wirklichkeit), *Reality (Re*alität), *Degrees of Being* (Seinsgrade).

The Extant *(Seiendes)* is the sum total of contrasts, and so it becomes the *actu ens.* The factor of Being, in the antithesis to possibility and factuality *(Wirklichkeit),* is, however, not identical with that of potency *(Potenz)* and act *(Akt),* of *dynamis* and *energeia.* Potency is predisposition to something. It leads to teleology, and in this respect the *energeia* precedes the *dynamis.* Once again we have to refer to Aristotle. On the other hand, possibility is the pure capability of Being.

But if we view the Extant as something real, while we do encounter a real possibility and a real necessity, we overlook the fact that there exists also an essential possibility and an essential necessity, and this is why we have once again missed the Extant as Extant. This is also why reality *(Realität)* is not the same as factuality *(Wirklichkeit)*. The latter comprises also the modalities of essence *(Wesen)*, while the former does not. There is an ideal Extant which is factual *(wirklich)* but not real.

It is advisable to establish some terminalogical conventions here. Possibility *(Möglichkeit)*, Factuality *(Wirklichkeit)* and Necessity *(Notwendigkeit)* will be referred to, each, as a *modus* (plural: *modi)*. For the Ideal *(Ideales)* and the Real *(Reales)* we reserve the expression *mode (Weise)*. On the other hand, concepts and classes, such as the Inorganic, the Organic, the Psychic and the Intellectual, will be called *strata (Schichten)*. Thus, there are modalities of Being, modes of Being, and strata of Being. The latter appear as peaks. For Neo-Platonism, matter was the non-extant, the spirit was pure Being, God the Super-Being — and this is a good example of the failure to understand Being. Popular metaphysics often does it the other way around. It seems something spectral in soul and spirit.

Being comprises all *modi* and modes, and here there are degrees of Being — but not in the case of the strata. Spiritual reality, too, is temporal, ephemeral and individual.

Chapter 9 — *Reflected Views of the Extant* (Seiendes).

These views take Being first as an intentional object, thus also that of fantasy, etc.; Husserl engaged in profound investigations on this topic. Next, as object of cognition, then as phenomenon, that-which-shows-itself. We have already mentioned the mistake made in this connection. The showing-itself is not an element of the Extant, but of the mode of givenness. There are also pseudo-phenomena.

Heidegger introduced the concept of accessibility (*Zuhandensein*) into ontogogy. This is the being of a utilitarian object for the existence (*Dasein*) of the user. Yet, everything that is a utilitarian object can also become an object of cognition — but not vice versa. In that case, the utilitarian object does not disappear, merely its utilitarian application does.

There is something unknown in every Extant, and this unknown is indicated in the problem of awareness. We call this "transobjective." Now then, if that which lies beyond the boundary is viewed as the true Being, this is the same error as the conferring of such dignity upon that which stands on this side of the boundary. A limit of objectification is made an essential limit. The same error re-occurs again — not with respect to that which is still unknown, but to that which remains unknowable. We do not call this "transobjective," but "transintelligible." It is the true Irrational. The Extant is indifferent to this cognitive limit — which is no limit of Being.

But the Extant proper can not only be shifted, as unknown or unknowable, in the natural direction, behind the object, but a shift may occur in the reverse direction, and the object may appear behind the subject. This produces the subject theories of the Extant. They assume the following forms: 1) The world, the not—I, the other I, are merely images in my mind. This comprises Fichte's subjective idealism, which believed that it had to take up the fight against the thing-in-itself. This comprises also solipsism, and many other things. — 2) A broad basis can be gained by an inclusion of the entire life of the Ego, as in Heidegger's concept of Hereness *(Dasein)*. The world is then the ever-mine. The basis has become broader, but the strictness of the former viewpoint has been sacrificed. — 3) The transsubjective and the transintelligible in the subject may, idealistically, form an unconscious and unknown background, or, realistically, may lead to the introduction of an *intellectus divinus, intuitivus et archetypus*. The inroad in the extended subject direction thus eventually does away with reflectivity itself — which was the origin of this movement.

Neo-Kantianism furnishes an example for the epistemological form of this error. It delves into a logical subject, a de-powered secondary Being, which it interprets as positive and predicative Being.

Chapter 10 — *The Limit of the Still-Not-Beyond Position* (Diesseitsstellung).

Now we have reached the extreme of subjective idealism, the immanence theory. Its proposition of consciousness states: Consciousness deals only with its images. It remains doubtful whether there are any corresponding material objects. This is the fountainhead of all scepticism. The immanance of intentional material objects becomes a prison. Up to now we were able to remain on this side of realism and idealism. But now this cannot go on. We are forced to decision.

We must discard the correlativistic prejudice. The oppositeness is not Being itself. The *intentio obliqua* must not be made the sole direction of sight. In the realm of cognition, every givenness of the Extant has the form of objecthood. The Being *per se (Ansichsein)* is a gnosiological concept, an epistemological line of separation, which serves a defensive purpose. Ontology has no need for it. The Being *per se* is superseded in the concept of the Extant as Extant.

It is no less wrong to say that "every Extant is a phenomenon." Not every Extant necessarily shows itself, and vice versa. The same holds true of the Extant and the material object. Givenness is just the beginning. Phenomena, too, have a Being, but not the Being of that which shows itself in them. The concept of something and the something of the concept possess two different types of Being. "Both are encompassed by the broad framework of the Extant. But it is no more possible to trace back Being *in genere* to the Being of the phenomenon than to trace it back to any other specific type of Being" (p. 87).

4

ON THE DIFFERENCE BETWEEN BEING (SEIN) AND EXTANT (SEIENDES)

Aristotle assigned to ontology (which he called also *philosophia prima,* and which his followers chose to name *metaphysics)* the task of understanding the Extant as Extant. Hartmann adopts this formula and shows its superiority to other formulations and definitions of tasks. He calls the "Extant as Extant" also *Extant as such* and *Being in general,* the latter expression being intended to indicate that sum total of the types of Extant which is the very factor that makes the Extant the Extant.

But this already calls for criticism.

Hartmann, too, knows that Extant and Being are not one and the same. But he puts the two all too close to each other. He fails to see the full difference which prevails here. In this respect, Heidegger is far superior to him. Aristotle's limitation consisted in the very fact that he adhered too strictly to the formula of Extant as Extant and failed to recognize the enormous difference from Being. This is why he lapsed into substantialism, and this is why he failed to see the difference between thing-in-itself *(Ding-an-sich)* and appearance *(Erscheinung)* in the Kantian sense, and treated the appearance as thing-in-itself. This should not be held against such an early thinker, by any means. But we ought to have got over that stage by now. It is true that Aristotle's formula is an excellent one and that it actually performs all the defensive motions which Hartmann ascribes to it and which he so brilliantly demonstrates about it — as that the taking of the Extant as merely apparent, as something in the state of becoming, ideated, subject-referred, shows that the formula, "Extant as Extant," has not been understood.

What, then, is the full difference between Extant and Being? Hartmann sees quite correctly that Being cannot be defined. It is impalpable. The statement that it is that which is a common property of various Extants is inadequate, too. It is based on that type of concept formation which brings out the abstract, general feature. This is no way to touch on Being. Being is incapable of definition for the very reason that it contains the source of the abstract and of the concrete as well. Being is no abstraction, nor is it an Extant. It is a prerequisite of both. Being is brought too close to the Extant if we fail to see in it that which, once lifted out of it, becomes the derived conceptual and abstract, and then has to confront the concretely extant. This is Hartmann's mistake. He approximates Being too close to the Extant. But then Being is only the common characteristic of the Extant as Extant in its manifold concrete manifestations. But how is such a characteristic of the common and general supposed to be ascribed to that which originally unites in itself this general with the concrete, and thus becomes the origin and source of this abstract generality? That which springs forth from the source is necessarily something else than the source itself. This is the difficulty of the comprehension of Being and the aporia of Being. The true task of ontology is not to understand the Extant as Extant, but to understand Being in its difference from the Extant as well.

Now then, this invokes something else again. Just because Being possesses this plus in differences compared with the Extant, which Hartmann no longer takes in consideration, the different moments of the act of comprehension are mutually interlinked in the comprehension of Being, *viz.*, a transcendent-realistic act and a transcendental-idealistic act. The two are inseparable, and no interpretation of Being is possible without them. They are an efficiently productive combination. Hartmann is not totally unaware of transcendental-idealistic acts, but he does not do them enough justice — for the very reason that he does not sufficiently distinguish between Being and Extant. Namely, the specific function of the transcendental-idealistic acts is to grasp the full import of this difference — that which is the source of the reflection, the *intentio obliqua*. It is therefore necessary to place very strong emphasis on the transcendental-idealistic factor, in opposition to Hartmann, in order to reach a truer and better understanding of Being. Hartmann lingers too much in the vicinity of the naive and natural-scientific world-view; this hampers his understanding of Being. The very *intentio obliqua* which he underestimates considerably, tries to move him away from it, to bring him the blessing, the fruits and results of the best modern philosophical efforts which have shouldered the burden of all the pains of reflection. But he does not allow them to do him this favor. He turns his back on all this — and therefore he loses sight of the best results and intellectual attitudes of modern philosophy. This is the reason why he partly falls behind Kant, and it is as though he were not even aware of the existence of Kant and his followers (who were not always as foolish as his views might make them appear). This is profoundly regrettable.

You cannot play the *intentio recta* and the *intentio obliqua* against each other. Both are good and necessary. But Hartmann plays the *intentio recta* against the *intentio obliqua*. To be sure, the opposite error must be just as carefully avoided. Modern phenomenology has achieved a part of its best results just because it has paid attention to the modes of attitude of the pre-predicative and natural-naive, and thus has done full justice to the *intentio recta,* without neglecting the *intentio obliqua.*

Hartmann believes that he takes a stand on this side of realism and idealism up to the end of the first treatise. It is only at the end of the first part that there appears a reason (subjective idealism) to warrant this stand. But this is wrong. By ascribing a predominant rôle to the Extant over Being, Hartmann has made a prejudgment which lands him right in the midst of preconceived dogmatism. He does not stand on this side of realism and idealism — he stands, from the very beginning, in the midst of transcendent realism toned down by a few trans-cendental-idealistic approaches. It is absolutely not neces-sary, or even possible, to seek such a non-dogmatic "this-side." This non-dogmatism is, paradoxically, a dogmatic attitude, itself. This follows from the nature of speak-ing and thinking. When we as much as open our mouths to give expression to something notional, we have always already reached a pre-conceived, dogmatic decision. Just because pure Being contains transcendent-realistic and transcendental-idealistic moments of under-standing within itself, every "this-side" of realism and idealism falls by the side. We always stand in one of the two or in both of them. If Being is gracious to us, it leads us to a harmonic understanding of its own self, which over-emphasizes neither the idealistic nor the realistic moments and moves in a beautiful mutual equilibrium of the *intentio recta* and the *intentio obliqua*. But, in this, we are heading toward a *Beyondness* with reference to realism and idealism. This is where Being, itself, stands. Not *this side* of both, but *beyond* both — or rather, the difference between "this side" and "beyond" becomes non-existent here. Being is the basic one-ness of both moments of understanding because it is the one-ness and the fountain-head of the concrete and of the abstract, of the Extant and of the cognitive view thereof.

In Section Two, we referred to the transcendental as the unknown X, and we faced the task of determining this X. We have now made a beginning toward this goal. But now the true X turns out to be Being, itself. It is distinguished by a non-definability and intangibility. It is therefore rightfully called X. The first definition consists in that it represents, essentially, the prime oneness of the transcendent-realistic and transcendentalidealistic views. And this is based on that prime one-ness of concrete and abstract, of Extant and views of Being, which is Being, itself. The view of Being appertains to Being no less than the Extant. The two relationships, however, are different from each other. The Extant is comprehended by the *intentio recta* in a naive perspective, natural science and science of the mind. The comprehension of Being asserts itself through all difficulties of reflection, of the abstract, of the formation of concepts, of the *intentio obliqua*, and builds on transcendentals. In this respect, however, we have not yet got past the beginnings, while the understanding of the

Extant is primeval. Ontology re-unites the two modes and reaches their prime one-ness. This is its only justification to bear its name.

As we have already found, Hartmann polemizes against Heidegger. Let us not go into details here. To be sure, it would be worth while to present a summary view of Heidegger's work, such as we attempt to give here of Hartmann's. Only then could we do him full justice, while expressing every justified criticism of his views, too. So long as this cannot be done, it would not be proper to slip in here a few precipitate comments on Hartmann's criticism of Heidegger. Hartmann must have failed to understand him fully — for Heidegger possesses far more understanding for the transcendental-idealistic moments of Being than Hartmann does. The way Heidegger contrasts Being with the Extant and refutes the blind adoption of the Aristotelian formula, is much nearer to the truth than are the conclusions of Hartmann. It is in this sense that Heidegger brings up again the problem of Being. He interprets the very fact of its decline onto the Extant as a sign of the profound oblivion of Being *(Seinsvergessenheit)* in which we live. A careful analysis of the available thoughts would be required in order to ascertain whether the necessary transcendent-realistic cognitive functions of Being are not slighted at that.

Heidegger's view of the world as the "ever-mine" must not be misconstrued as the dictum of an empirical subjectivism as it seems to be done by Hartmann. Heidegger's existential analysis of "Being-in-the-World" *(In-der-Welt-Sein)* takes the transcendence problem very seriously. But he treats it with tools of the transcendental method, and therefore the "ever-mine" is also a transcendental "ever-mine." To be sure, Heidegger wants to understand the finiteness of man, and nothing further. But by that he sets limits for himself — not with respect to philosophy, but to theology. As mentioned, only a very detailed investigation could furnish a true, objective picture and judgment.

But we can state this much: Heidegger does not de-power the objective spirit, nor does he make the stratum of Being of the historical spirit impalpable. The brilliant analysis of historism in *Sein und Zeit* alone is sufficient to demonstrate this, and it is demonstrated even more by the later researches of Heidegger, his relationship to Dilthey, etc. Moreover: The query for Being is necessarily also a query for the meaning of Being. It is more than that, but it is this, too, and quite essentially so. And just because it is also interlined with the query for the Being of meaning, there exists after all a meaning *per se,* even though this Being *per se (Ansichsein)* is transcendental-idealistic, and not transcendent-realistic.

It may be helpful now to make a basic stipulation about the concepts *transcendent* and *transcendental.* The two are not synonymous; between them, they denote an extreme contrast. Our cognition, as seen quite correctly by Hartmann, is naturally directed at its object. It forgets and loses itself in it. In order to pay heed to the cognition itself and to make it an object, reflection is required, and this confronts thinking with immeasurable difficulties — which, however, are not self-made, but mostly genuine problems. Of course, there are some pseudo-problems mixed in with them, too. Psychology and logic show similar elements of reflection. Everything that pertains to the background, which now lies in the direction leading to the object, can be called "transcendent." Hartmann points out two varieties of it: the unknown or transobjective, and the irrational or transintelligible on the side of the object. This is how it appears from the transcendental-idealistic point of view. However, transcendent-realistically, that which is known and understood, that which lies "on this side" of the cognitive limit (which is no limit of Being), pertains to the transcendent, while the latter is immanent from the transendental-idealistic point of view, in the sense of the appearance as against the thing-in-itself, which alone is the truly transcendent in the proper sense of the term. This is what Hartmann calls the transintelligible or the irrational.

But a similar background element showed up in the direction toward the subject, too. Something that is transsubjective can only be unknown at the present time, and so far, from the transcendental-idealistic point of view, it pertains to the appearance and its immanence. But the subject contains also an eternally irrational and transintelligible element. Now then, everything that is background-toned toward the subject is *transcendental,* as distinguished from *transcendent.* This is but a first and still incomplete definition. But this is only the beginning of the elucidation of the two concepts.

Kant calls that cognition "transcendental" which *a priori* covers theoretically an entire range of another *a priori* cognition as to its possibility. Thus, the theory of space and time was a transcendental knowledge, because it permits the *a priori* comprehension of the possibilities of geometry and algebra as fields of cognition. This concept of the transcendental therefore differs both from the empirical and from the *aprioristical,* which becomes the concern of the transcendental. On the other hand, Kant contrasts the concept "transcendent" with "immanent." He uses it especially to distinguish the ephemeral pseudo-cognition of rational metaphysics. But this makes "transcendental" an antithesis of "transcendent" in his philosophy, too.

All this makes it understandable that transcendental realism is a contradiction in itself — from the viewpoint of the Extant only. Realism can only be either transcendent or immanent-empirical. The latter is relatively meaningless, while transcendent realism is a meaningful and characterful phenomenon.

It is a different story with idealism, and this denotes its broader range. It can be transcendent, transcendental and immanent-empirical-subjectivistic. The latter is the one-sided extreme to transcendent realism pure and simple. Transcendent idealism is an aberration. One of its forms is, for instance, hylozoism. Transcendental idealism alone is, in turn, a necessary and characterful phenomenon, worthy friend and foe of transcendent realism. Both are combined in the genuine understanding of Being, both serve it, and both want to express themselves in ontology. But, then, the discovery of what the transcendental really is and means, becomes a new task. The above-cited definitions of the transsubjective are very rudimentary, incomplete, and partly even outright wrong. However, it is the transcendental that displays a penetration through the subject. But this is still not all. It is quite impossible to state as yet just what else there is. In part, it has not been discovered as yet. We are in the first stages of this quest, a hunt for noble game. This is part and parcel of the particular nature of the transcendental, so strongly in contrast to the Extant and to the transcendent. Even that which transcendent-realistically pertains to the irrational and transintelligible can be still fathomed transcendentally. The transcendent-realistic irrational is not the end of the ways of the transcendental. The decision on this is objectively anticipated in the pure Being.

Reflection is the very thing that reaches farther than merely to the object or even to the Extant. It penetrates deep enough to touch on Being, and this is its significant rôle in philosophy. In the midst of the reflected deliberation to hold fast to the awareness of it, the understanding of Being is the only starting point for the accomplishment of it. For in Being, the transcendent-realistic and transcendental-idealistic moments prevail already. That which phenomenology touches is already the true thing, but not yet the *whole* thing. So long as the thing can still be distinguished from the phenomena of the thing, phenomenology still has further transcendental investigations to perform. To be sure, as it proceeds further, it ceases being phenomenology. It gets ahead of itself and becomes something else — for the very reason that it attains to a deeper grasp of the transcendental. To be sure, bracketing, reduction and raising before the bracket are methods of the exploration of essentialities *(Wesenheiten)* which cannot suffice for long.

Hartmann proffers significant propositions containing the word "indifferent" *(gleichgültig)*. We might call these his "indifference propositions." It is important to query their true meaning and to check them over. Thus, the Extant is indifferent to the limit of objectification, indifferent to whether or not it is understood for what it is, whether or not it is a material object, whether it is irrational or rational. Now then, this is indubitably so in the realm of transcendent realism, and this very viewpoint demonstrates something of true Being — although this something is already a decay product, related to the other decay product of subjective idealism of the immanence of awareness, and of abstractism. This indifference applies to the Extant, but not to Being, and this is another evidence of the harm wrought by letting the Extant outweigh Being. Being is not indifferent to the limit of objectification, to the givenness, to the alternative of being known or ignored, to that of the rational or irrational, etc. — the selfsame Being which is the Being of the Extant, the transcendent-realistic comprehension of which as an Extant is limited to a one-sided aspect of its essence. The indifference propositions of Hartmann are wrong, because they overlook the transcendental constituent in Being, and admit it only in a diluted form. Being is *also* the pure yielding and self-display of the Extant. Once again, Heidegger goes farther here with his interpretation of the truth, of the *a-letheia,* as the state of non-concealment. In view of this, it is true in a very subordinate sense only that the Extant is indifferent to whether it shows itself or not. Not every Extant shows itself, and not everything that shows itself is an Extant. It holds true within the framework of the transcendent-realistic partial understanding of Being through understanding of the Extant. This does not carry far. It is wrong in the sense of the strict understanding of Being, which touches on the ultimate. The Being of the Extant is an unfathomable mystery. For this very reason, we must not reject anything that may prove expedient for us in any manner. It is wonderful to think that there exists here a constructive cooperation between the transcendent-realistic and transcendental-idealistic outlooks. The natural sciences and the sciences of the mind keep making steady progress in the revealing of the Extant as Extant. Philosophy, epistemology, psychology, logic, metaphysics and ontology open up ever newer depths of the transcendental. A transcendental subject and similar concepts are certainly no last word here. But they are way-stations along the right road. And if we have done all we could, and if we have absorbed the entire wealth of historical findings, we still have merely scooped up one single drop from an ocean. This is what Being, the great mystery, is like. It seems to be an abstraction, and yet it is not one. It is the Being of the Extant, and the Extant is unable to grasp it mentally. But this very enigmatic feature engenders more insight than the obvious, and it leads to an unlimited progress of scientific and philosophical cognition.

Also the value theory is more transcendentally than realistically toned. At any rate, evil is no less existing than goodness, and Being knows no relative degrees. But it may be that evil is evil because it is the extant evil, that therefore the ethical-qualitative distinction of good and evil has something to do with the difference between Being and Extant, which Hartmann fails to emphasize sufficiently. We shall investigate this question more closely when analyzing Hartmann's ethics, which he expounded in a bulky volume. In the direction of transcendentalization there is something valuable that cannot be comprehended transcendent-realistically. This is where the value theory wants to start out.

The realm of ideal essentialities, universals with their timelessness and perpetuality, has attracted philosophical thought since time immemorial. Today, we know that they, too, miss Being, because they are the fruit of a separation from a whole which combines the *essentia* and the *existentia* within Being as an original unit. Quiddity and haecceity are absurd and unnatural ways and tools for a cognition of the radication of the "thus-extant" *(soseiend)* individual element in Being. Existence *(Existenz)* is like a transcendental positing with respect to the essence *(Essenz)*. Kant makes use of this insight in order to destroy the ontological proof of the existence of God. There is a cognition of the *That (Dass)* that reaches deeper than the comprehension of the *What (Was)* that furnishes a foundation to the latter and achieves a more solid insight into the Extant. And this is certainly capable also of being instrumental in the interpretation of Being. But nominalism will then not be the reverse of this existentialism. If it were, it would be bought at too high a price, and this would be still another instance where a one-sidedness, a particularism would arise, out of the mistake of substituting a decay product for Being and of being unable to espy the original in the secret of Being. Only a corrupted awareness of Being can spawn forth such notions. It is the task of modern ontology to restore the corrupted awareness of being to its wholesome state. It is rich, tender and sensitive. Being has a history that is nothing less than fantastic, as fascinating as life itself.

If this book is to have a sequel, we shall have still the opportunity to treat of the modalities at length, for Hartmann authored a special treatise dedicated to them exclusively. Let it suffice here to say that possibility-reality-necessity is more helpful in the comprehension of Being than the Aristotelian substitute, potentiality-actuality. Those pure modalities display a preponderance of the transcendental, while the latter antithetical couplet represents more the transcendent-realistic departure in the investigation of modalities. The fact that Aristotle places *energeia* before *dynamis* as an essential premise of the latter, shows an instinctive appreciation of the transcendental, for which at that time no explicit formula could be found as yet. The first-mentioned view of reality embraces both Real Possibility-Real

Necessity *(Realmöglichkeit-Realnotwendigkeit)* and Essential Possibility-Essential Necessity *(Wesensmöglichkeit-Wesensnotwendigkeit)*. There is a similar relationship between the transcendent-realistic and the transcendental-idealistic. The sum of the two points at the preceding unit — Being, which is no more than an abstract, universal general and a collective Being *on* the Extant. Being in this sense is like a prolific nil, X, impalpable and intangible, and hence the Being *per se (Sein für sich)* and the Extant *per se (das Seiende für sich)*, the abstract and the concrete, are already decay products — decomposition products, in fact. The modalities touch on this secret conceptually and categorically. Therefore, the Extant as something merely real, and — in the language of translation — Being as Reality, is merely an incomplete paraphrase of Being. The fine distinction between Reality *(Realität)* and Factuality *(Wirklichkeit)* is that the latter encompasses also the Ideal, while the former does not. Something that is an Extant ideally, can be factual *(wirklich)*, but it is not *(real)*. That which is Extant really, is factual and real. Of course, a one-sided preference for the essential possibility-essential necessity couplet would amount to the same mistake, in the opposite direction. Being as ideality, too, is only an incomplete paraphrasing. The doctrine of the *essentia* could not avoid this error.

Three such different determinants of Being as the modalities of Being *(Seinsmodalitäten)*, modes of Being *(Seinsweisen)*, and strata of Being *(Seinsschichten)*, are necessary in order to warrant a more complete definition of Being, and even then the problem of the unity of Being as X is still untouched, If Neo-Platonism calls matter the "non-extant," spirit the "pure Being," God the "Super-Extant," this is just a sign of the fine sense necessary for an incipient understanding of Being. He who is capable of forming a first inkling of the meaning of Being, must regard such a materialistic and substantialistic treatment of Being as a frivolous play. Being encompasses the *modi,* the modes and the strata. But this is still not all of it.

In Chapter Nine, Hartmann resumes his criticism of Heidegger — this time in connection with "accessibility" *(Zuhandenheit).* But here, too, we must rally to Heidegger's defense. The analysis of accessibility in the light of the type of Being of utilitarian objects, tools and other implements, is after all just a prelude to the rest. The utilitarian object is evaluated later also as to its Being as object of cognition, first as a deficient *modus,* but later on positively, too. We cannot go into any more details here.

It is to be stated, with respect to a further point of criticism, that the difference between Heidegger and subjective idealism, which makes the world an image in the subject's mind, is not merely that Heidegger, at the cost of strict accuracy, invested this fundamental thesis with a broader basis; the difference is that Heidegger brought out transcendental-idealistic moments of Being which are missing in subjective idealsm. The difference is qualitative, not quantitative.

The metaphysical subject, the transcendental subject, the unconscious and unknown world background, the *intellectus divinus, intuitivus et archetypus,* the logical subject of the positing and of predicative Being, are certainly poor, incomplete and partly erroneous views of the transcendental element in Being. But only partly so. One must not "pour out the child with the bath." All these attempts at comprehension display also genuine transcendental-idealistic moments of Being, which must be put in bold relief. They show truth on the march. In exculpation of these partly childishly naive, abortive attempts, attention must be called to the enormous difficulty of the investigation.

The correlativistic subject-object relationship becomes a prejudice, owing to the very fact that the Extant tends to overshadow Being. In Being, itself, this correlativism changes over into something else that limits it and makes it relative, and thus reduces it to its true proportion. The extant subject has the same mode of Being as the extant object, but the subjective view of Being has another mode of Being. The "something" of a concept is different from the concept of "something." But there are also exceptions, such as, for instance, the concept of the "act of thinking." It is only when Being and its two main moments are seen simultaneously that the synopsis takes place which turns all possibilities of Being into a genuine specification.

5

THE RELATIONSHIP OF HERENESS (DASEIN) AND SUCHNESS (SOSEIN)

The above phrase is the title of Part Two of the *Grundlegung* (pp. 88-150). It is, in turn, subdivided into threee Sections. Section One is entitled, *Die Aporetic von "Dass"* und *"Was"* (The Aporia of the *"That"* and the *"What"*).

Chapter 11 — *Reality* (Realität) and *Existence* (Existenz).

A more complete list of the indifference of the Extant to its specific attributes is as follows: Substance-accidence, unity-manifoldness, determinacy-indeterminacy, matter-form, value-disvalue, individuality-universality, individual-universe, part-whole, element-system, subject-object, person-thing, world-human being, apparent-non-apparent, objectified-transobjective, rational-irrational, absolute-relative, independent-dependent, simple-compound, lower structure-higher structure. The Extant as Extant is indifferent to all these differences.

On the other hand, the situation is different with respect to the following antitheses: *Essentia-existentia, suchness-hereness (Sosein-Dasein),* factuality-possibility (*Wirklichkeit-Möglichkeit*), real-ideal. The Extant as

Extant is not indifferent to these. This remarkable fact calls for explanation. The traditional concepts of these antithesis show discrepancies.

Existence (*Existenz*) is bare in a certain sense — the bare "that something *is*." Reality *(Realität)* stands for more than bare existence. That which is real is temporal and individual. On the other hand, there is also an ideal existence. For this reason, the *essentia* cannot be identified forthwith with the ideal. Essentialities (*Wesenheiten*) are no realm existing for themselves; they occur *in* something extant, and this is what facilitates the delusion by this identification. The *essentia* does not encompass the entire structural suchness *(Sosein)* of an Extant, but merely that which is essential, in contrast to that which is non-essential — which, too, is a part of the structural suchness. This becomes the source of further ambiguities. The accidental suchness *(Sosein)* belongs to the state-of-being-configurated *(Geformtsein)* — in other words, not to the existence; the latter is the bare *That,* which naturally never occurs as such.

The essentialities *(Wesenheiten)* occur in the real world; therefore, they must possess a certain congruity with ideal Being. Mathematical Being, and also the values are ideal, without belonging to the *essentia.* The realm of the ideal is thus broader than that of the es-*sentia.*

The *existentia* is the *That,* the *essentia* is the *What,* the quiddity of the Extant. Let us replace the historic-ally overworked couple of concepts, *essentia-existentia,* by the pair, *suchness-hereness (Sosein-Dasein).* Suchness is reflected better by the quiddity than by the *essentia,* because the quiddity has absorbed everything that is accidental, while the *essentia* excludes it. Also the ideal has its being *(Bestehen)*, its factual existence or hereness *(Dasein)*.

The old ontology emphasized the severance of hereness and suchness. The severance is treated in the next Chapter.

Chapter 12 — The Severance of Hereness (Dasein) *and Suchness* (Sosein).

The distinction becomes a severance which subdivides the world. Suchness *(Sosein)* is superimposed onto that which has hereness *(das Daseiende)*; it is indifferent to existence *(Existenz)*, and existence is indifferent to suchness.

The *essentia* was linked with the definition, and thus a logical theory of the *essentia* was developed. In fact, there are judgments of suchness *(Sosein)* and judgments of hereness *(Dasein)*. The simplest formulas for this purpose are *S is P*, and *S is*. In this process, the *a priori* method of cognition was assigned to suchness (*Sosein*), and the *a posteriori* method was earmarked for the cognition of hereness *(Dasein)*, but it was admitted at the same time that cognition of suchness could be attained by the *a posteriori* method, too. The cognition of universality and of laws encompasses principally the suchness. Individual cases are left open; they remain a gap. Existence as hereness *(Dasein)* alone is real.

This leads to fine metaphysical points. Of the Kantian thing-in-itself *(Ding-an-sich)*, only the *That* is recognized, not the *What*. Suchness belongs to the appearance. It is a *Being-for-us (Für-uns-sein)*. The suchness *(Sosein)* is *in mente*, the hereness *(Dasein)* is *extra mentem*. This is how Scheler interprets Kant. But he is mistaken. Kant, of all people, was aware of the fact that things-in-themselves have their unrecognized suchness (*Sosein*). He did not take the limitation of knowledge for a limit of Being. And this is how also the hereness (*Dasein*) occurs *in mente*. In *mente* and *extra mentem* are not mutually contradictory. A similar error was committed by nominalism, too, in that it saw that the *universalia post res* exist in the conscious awareness, while it overlooked the fact that this does not preclude the *"in rebus."*

The *existentia* has no privileged position; it is not actuality. Suchness (*Sosein*) has its hereness (*Dasein*) in the things, but it is the same hereness as that of the things.

Chapter 13 — Repeal of the Severance.

There can be no cognition of the suchness (*Sosein*) without the hereness (*Dasein*), and so suchness is believed to have no existence. There is a suchness of the non-existent, and this leads to the error of confusing the cognitive limit of knowledge with the limit of Being. That which is meant is always the suchness of existing cases, even if they cannot always be ascertained.

There is something gnosiologically irritating in *a priori* knowledge. Hereness (*Dasein*) can only be known *a posteriori*, suchness (*Sosein*), on the other hand, *a priori*, by a knowledge of law and form. But Kant restricted the validity of the pure intellectual concepts to the field of possible experience. *A priori* knowledge, therefore, cannot be isolated. We possess no intuitive understanding. In connection with the *a priori* ideal cognition there are *per se* no individual instances; here, suchness and hereness are truly not severed. The ontological antithesis of hereness and suchness does not coincide with the gnosiological antithesis of a *posteriori* and *a priori*.

Capacity of being defined, too, is an uneven yard-stick, for the antithesis of the logical and alogical represents no existential borderline. Even in the famous Kantian argument concerning the one hundred coins, the "mine-ness" can be included in the definition when Kant says that the existence or non-existence of the one hundred coins means a difference in *my* possession, even though the fact of existence does not add anything to the essence content. There is no such thing in the world as bare general hereness *(Dasein);* it is merely a border-line case. Suchness and specific hereness become relative in the Extant itself.

Chapter 14 — The Types of Judgment and their Translatability.

Judgments of hereness *(Daseinsurteile)* can be translated into judgments of suchness *(Sosein)*. "S is" is logically equivalent to "*S is extant*" or "*S is existing*"; thus it has the form, "*S is P.*" The word *is* is ambiguous. It means the predicative content of Being the *esse praedicativum,* the copula, and it also expresses existence *(Existenz)*. Judgments of suchness *(Sosein)* and hereness *(Dasein)* only differ in logical form, not ontologically. An assertion of hereness *(Dasein)* may be bare or relative.

This is why, inversely, also the judgments of suchness can be translated into judgments of hereness. In this respect, it is unimportant that this is often feasible solely by a linguistic artificiality, for language is to serve practical purposes. "The table is square" and "The table has four corners" are judgments of suchness. The corresponding judgments of hereness are: "There are four corners on the table," and "The four corners of the table *are* (exist)." The content of the predicative Being is identical in both cases. To be sure, nobody will express as quoted in our fourth example — but this is immaterial. *"S is P,"* therefore, means *"there is P in S."* The suchness has been translated into hereness. This reducibility is reciprocal. This logical survey warrants the hope that suchness and hereness might be mutually inter-convertible in the Extant as Extant, too. The aim now is to demonstrate this.

Section II — Ontically Positive Relationship of Hereness (Dasein) and Suchness (Sosein)

Chapter 15 — Repeal of the Ontological Semblance

The substratum category is responsible for a misuse. Hereness *(Dasein)* is no vehicle, no substance, but a mode of Being *(Seinsweise)*. The entire Extant splits into the two modes of Being — real and ideal hereness. Hereness *(Dasein)* and existent *(Daseindes)* apply to substance *and* to attributes.

Contemplated from the viewpoint of suchness, hereness appears to be accidental. This line runs all the way through suchness, splitting it into the essential and the non-essential. But it is only when seen from the viewpoint of essential necessity that the accidental character of hereness, as against suchness, becomes evident — not from the viewpoint of real necessity. The two modalities are mistaken for each other, and this is how the semblance is born.

Suchness appears as indifferent toward hereness (its antithesis) only if suchness is understood as ideal Being, and hereness as real Being. But the Real has suchness, and the Ideal has hereness. Once again, we gain a glimpse here into the witches' kitchen which is semblance.

Hereness changes with its attributes. The indifference ends within the same mode of Being. The chorism of the moments of Being vanishes. Indifference exists only among the moments of *different* spheres of Being.

Chapter 16 — The Errors in the Modal Argument

A deceptive "sleight-of-mind" is practiced with possibility and factuality *(Wirklichkeit)*. Suchness *(Sosein)* appears as possible Being, and hereness *(Dasein)* as actual Being. The doctrine of Leibniz of possible worlds in the mind of God, of which He chose the best one, and the already mentioned argument of Kant of the one hundred possible coins, are good examples. Possibility here means contradiction-proofness. It is the product of the other sphere of the mere thought content. Both examples lack the realizing principle, which, *e. g.*, in the Kantian example would be the work which endow the possible one hundred coins with factuality *(Wirklichkeit)*. The point is that essential possibility is something quite different from real possibilty. The moments of Being termed *hereness* and *suchness,* and the spheres of Being termed *reality* and *ideality,* overlap the modes of Being termed *actuality* and *possibility* — and vice-versa. Careful distinction must therefore be made among four totally different instances of possibility, and the same number of instances of actuality. Confusion of these instances engender errors, such as the fundamental severance of suchness and hereness.

Chapter 17 — Conjunctive and Distinctive Antithesis

Hereness *(Dasein)* and suchness *(Sosein)* are different (although not separate), but "existent" *(Daseiendes)* and "so-existent" *(Soseiendes)* are one and the same Extant *(Seiendes)*, displaying the effects of two moments. Suchness is indifferent toward ideality and reality, insofar as these two mutually coincide, and this is what we call neutral suchness *(neutrales Sosein)*.

This makes the sphere difference of Real and Ideal an antithesis as to mode of hereness. The ontic weight rests on the hereness. The suchness links the two spheres, hereness separates them.

Thus there is a conjunction of the moments of Being (hereness and suchness) and a disjunction of the modes of Being (real and Ideal). Here, the difference between real and ideal Being is the difference between the modes of hereness. The difference between hereness and suchness is the difference between the mode of Being and the definiteness of Being. For there is no neutral hereness. This difference between real and ideal Being is the difference in mode of hereness. But since suchness is neutral, the mode of Being exists in the mode of hereness. There is no neutral "so-extant" *(Soseiendes)*; there is only a neutral suchness *(Sosein)*. Moreover, there is no real "existent" *(Daseiendes)* that is not a real "so-extant" *(Soseiendes.)*

Let us tabulate the four possibilities in the following order:

Ideal suchness *(Sosein)*	Ideal hereness *(Dasein)*
Real suchness *(Sosein)*	Real hereness *(Dasein)*

The horizontal row shows the conjunctive relationship, the vertical column shows the disjunctive relationship. There is also a good sense in replacing, on the left side, the ideal and real suchness by a neutral suchness, but the union of ideal suchness with ideal hereness in an ideal Being leads to the fatal mistakes which we have revealed. Already the best solution in the battle over the universals trained its sights on the neutral suchness, without a clear recognition of the character of the latter.

It plays a part in modern phenomenology, too. That which is "de-bracketed," in the sense of Husserl, is basically the neutral suchness. In this connection, it is not a question of the Ideal, but of the essentialities (*Wesenheiten*).

Section III—The Inner Relationship of the Moments of Being
Chapter 18—*Hereness* (Dasein) *in the Suchness* (Sosein) *and Suchness in the Hereness*

The relationship of the moments of Being contains a link and a relativity. The mode of Being and the hereness are indifferent to the difference between substantive and adjective Being. There exists a relativization of the *That* and the *What,* which displays a contrast in direction. The *P*-ness of *S* means also that the total relation, "*S* is *P*," is an extant one. There is a character of hereness in suchness itself, and vice-versa. This can be demonstrated on the Extant as Extant, itself, and this is what we intend to do now.

Chapter 19 — *Sameness and Unlikeness of the Moments of Being*

The whole of the interrelationship of Being houses a continually shifting sameness of hereness and suchness. Every suchness of something is the hereness of something else, and vice-versa. Examples: The hereness of the tree is the suchness of the forest, the hereness of the twig is the suchness of the tree, the hereness of the leaf is the sushness of the twig, the hereness of the vein is the suchness of the leaf. Now then, this holds true inversely, too: The suchness of the leaf is the hereness of the vein, the suchness of the branch is the hereness of the leaf, etc. In the world as a whole, the relationship approaches sameness. It is a continually shifting sameness, *Essentia* is also *existentia,* and vice-versa.

Suchness is the hereness of something "in" something. The difference between free and bound existence *(Existenz)* is ontical, but it is a difference in suchness, not in hereness. Everything that exists has its *Where, Wherein* and *Whereby,* and this itself is existent in the same sense.

The range of sameness of suchness and hereness reaches as far as the first member; this becomes especially clear when applied to the pattern of causality. This is, then, where the ontic borderline lies. The way proceeding from hereness to suchness runs into an upper limit — the world as a whole. Its hereness is no longer the suchness of something else.

It is a directional difference in the identity shift; the direction is irreversible. The contrast of the moments of Being holds something over that does *not* melt into the shift of identity, as have seen in the example of the world as a whole, and a residue of the predominant rôle shifts onto the side of hereness. Hereness contains the mode of Being.

Chapter 20 — *The Result and its Consequences*

Every suchness is a hereness, and every hereness is a suchness. The individual Extant always carries the mark of both. There is no neutral Extant. The semblance of severance has an ontologic basis, which is no semblance. Suchness is the adherence to something, whereas hereness seems to be unbound. The semblance that the vehicle extant in itself has no suchness, and that suchness has no hereness, lingers on even after it has been unmasked. Actually, things-in-themselves do have a suchness, only not that of the phenomena, and the suchness does have hereness, although it is difficult to recognize it. A highly developed reflection is required for all this. The epistemological basis of the severance is that hereness is only given *a posteriori,* while suchness is accessible to *a priori* cognition, too. This is why the two seem to exist separately, especially if the material object *(Gegenstand)* as something objectified is not distinguished from the Extant as Extant *(Seiendes).*

Chapter 21 — *Modes of Givenness* (Gegebenheitsweisen) *and Modes of Being* (Seinswesen)

The findings can be summed up in five sentences:

1 — The following are open to *a priori* cognition: Ideal suchness *(Sosein),* ideal hereness *(Dasein),* and real suchness. Real hereness is beyond the range of *a priori* cognition.

2 — Real suchness and real hereness are accessible to the *a posteriori* method. This method cannot be applied to ideal suchness and ideal hereness.

3 — Real suchness alone is accessible both to *a priori* and *a posteriori* cognition.

4 — Real hereness is accessible to *a posteriori* cognition only.

5 — Every ideal Being *(Sein),* whether ideal suchness or ideal hereness, is accessible to *a priori* cognition only.

However, real hereness can indirectly be made accessible to *a priori* cognition — namely, to *a priori* cognition which is not pure *a priori* cognition, in which connection it is still an open question to what extent the latter exists at all.

The basis of the semblance of the splitting of Being is that the cognition is split. This follows from the pattern of our organization. The semblance is produced by reflection — by the epistemological reflection in particular.

6

MODES AND MODALITIES OF BEING

The fundamental relationship is that of Being *(Sein)* and Extant *(Seiendes)*. First of all, on the side of Being, a distinction is made here between abstract and concrete Being. The former is the Being defined by the formation as an essentiality *(Wesenheit)*, whereas under the latter aspect the Extant appears as thing, essence, substance, vehicle and substratum. For this Extant, then, the transcendent-realistic view predominates and becomes particularly dominant in the naive outlook and in natural science. Hartmann's entire ontology remains close to this type. Abstract Being is the start of that transcendental-idealistic view of the Extant which discovers the transcendental through reflection.

This start wants to develop and to progress. The more it does so, the more thorough is the repeal of the difference between realism and idealism. This is how concrete Being develops, and under this definition also the Extant changes its countenance. Being does not cease now to be the Being of the Extant, as the abstract Being was. This remains and represents a common feature of abstract and concrete Being. The difference between the two consists, rather, in that the Extant becomes assimilated to Being — that it becomes more and

57

more Being-like. Concrete Being is the fruit of the fully developed transcendental, in which abstract Being and Extant, the ideal and the real, *a priori* and *a posteriori,* the transcendent-realistic and the transcendental-idealistic, blend in a union defined by concrete Being itself. A process of concretization has set in, which finds its fulfillment in concrete Being.

We see that in this view and conceptual definition of concrete Being, modes of Being are linked with modes of cognition and of givenness. This is because the latter, too, are modes of Being, deeper than the first modes of Being, the first Ideal and the first Real. They are modes of Being that reveal the Extant-in-itself *(Ansichseiendes)* element of the Extant *(Seiendes)* — modes of Being *per se* *(Ansichsein).* All the pains of reflection are not suffered in vain. They deliver this valuable fruit. This Being *per se,* these modes of Being of the transcendental which constitute concrete Being, manifest themselves first on the Extant — on the corporeal, hypostatic, substantial, essential and substratic Extant, the Being of which is not the concrete but the abstract Being, itself as an Extant, namely as a thing-in-itself *(Ding-an-sich)* or as many things-in-themselves, and this shifts the emphasis on the first concept, on appearance, the fact-of-being-appearance, the extant appearance, as distinguished from the thing-in-itself. Kant still moves in the range of this concept formation, although he does present higher motives at the same time. According to Kant, the thing-in-itself is the absolute, ultimate unknown. Unity and plurality, existence or hereness, or even suchness (as Hartmann thinks that there are many things-in-themselves with an unknown or unknowable suchness) cannot be referred to the thing-in-itself. For all these terms are categories, and they apply merely to the appearance, and not to the thing-in-itself. Hartmann's interpretation of the Kantian thing-in-itself is, therefore, as un-Kantian as can be. It involves not *an* error, but *many* errors. It is wrong to ascribe an unknown or unknowable suchness (!) to many (!!) things-in-themselves, citing in evidence the solidity of the Extant which is indifferent to cognition and cognitive limits, and to refuse to let these be limits of Being. It is wrong — firstly, because this solidity of Being is fully true already in the extant appearance, which is not the thing-in-itself; secondly, because existence, suchness and plurality can not be ascribed at all to things-in-themselves; thirdly, because the cognitive limits to be considered here are limits of Being at the same time (the two are by no means mutually contradictory) and not merely something gnosiological, but also something ontological, which opens up the very depths of the Extant. The fourth and most valid reason, however, is that the thing-in-itself does not pertain to the Extant at all, but to Being. To be sure, the limit of Kantian thinking becomes manifest here, and this limit must be passed — but not by doing away with the transcendental-idealistic in Kant, as Hartmann would, but by the very opposite method — by developing it further. Turning Kant into a one-sided transcendent-realist means diluting Kant. Concrete Being, itself, is the true Being *per se* of the Extant. Its contribution to abstract Being reveals the deepest aspects of the Extant. The Extant becomes Being-toned. Being *per se* overcomes the apearance and fills it out, becomes its *pleroma*. The difference between appearance and thing-in-itself goes by the board, because abstract Being and *its* Extant are united. The transcendental — concrete Being — shows the presence of Real and Ideal, of hereness and suchness, of *a priori* and *a posteriori*. This is what makes manifest the most profound motives for the division of the Extant into appearance and thing-in-itself, and shows what the commingling and confusion of the two really means.

The selfsame factor which makes Being abstract and essence-like, makes also the Extant particular, transcendent-realistic, hypostatic, substantial, substratic, and highlights its Being and its existence as reality as opposed to ideality. And the selfsame factor that makes Being concrete and super-essential, dehypostates also the Extant, takes away its particularity, unites the transcendent-realistic with the transcendental-idealistic, loosens up its substantiality and substraticity, assimilates it to Being and existence, leads to a filling up and fulfillment of reality as converging toward ideality. This transcendentalization is concrete Being itself, and it runs through all reflection. The Extant of the abstract Being is transcendent, as the latter is immanent. But in concrete Being, transcendence and immanence become meaningless because they become something new. This "something new" is concrete Being, itself, which is the Being of the Being-ful Extant (*das seinshaft Seiende*). This holds the key to the solution of the epistemological problem at the same time. In concrete Being, the essence is incorporated, absorbed into existence, structural suchness into the hereness. In this sense, concrete Being is neutral.

Being is partly identical with existence. The latter is the pure, bare *That*. We have seen already in the logical judgment that "*S is*" is equivalent to "*S exists*," and in this sense we say that existence is Being. The entire existence is identical with Being — but not vice-versa. Being encompasses more than pure, bare existence. This is why we have stated that Being is partly identical with existence. That which makes Being more than existence, is like a garment that covers its bareness. Existence is amplified in Being.

In abstract Being, Being and existence are still mutually contrasted. For abstract Being is essenceful. It has existence in the sense of a secondary, allusive concept formation. It *is* not yet truly the existence of the extant; it is existence solely in the sense of *What-ness* — in other words, in the very sense contrasted to existence, as *essentia* against *existentia*. But an existential moment is already present. *"S is P"* means also: *"the P-ness of the S exists."* A concretization sets in now, in the course of which Being becomes more and more existence proper, in that at the same time it "dresses up" the latter. Concrete Being is pleromatic existence. The Being of *"S is"* in the sense of *"S exists"* is, therefore, the Being of an intermediate stage between the abstract and the concrete Being which has added to the *What-ness* the positedness of the *What-ness*. This absolute position of existence is, as mode of giveness, the decisive mode of Being of existence itself. It is an unfolding of Being.

As for existence, we distinguish *Existence (Existenz)*, *Existent (das Existierende)*, and *Fact-of-Existing (Existieren)*. In the case of Being *(Sein)*, we have no three terms, but just two: the Extant *(das Seiende)* corresponds to the Existent — it is the extant Existent and the existent Extant. But Being corresponds to Existence and also to the Fact-of-Existing, although more to the former. We shall reserve this expression in our terminology for its correspondence to Existence. But, then, we need another expression to designate that which in the sphere of Being would correspond to the Fact-of-Existing. We suggest the word *hereness (Dasein)* for this use. To a certain extent, these are matters of a wise and expedient terminological convention. The main thing is to adhere to the system once it has been established.

So, the fact of the existence of the extant Existent will be called its *hereness (Dasein)* (*). That-which-exists *(Daseiendes)* is, then, the existent Extant. It is *"here"* and *"now."* Hereness *(Dasein)* might perhaps be called more expediently *Now-Being (Jetztsein)*, but in the predicative view space often stands for time. The *here (da)* is a spatial element.

Hereness (Dasein) and *That-ness (Dass-sein)* are not one and the same thing. The former is the Fact-of-Existing *(Existieren)*, the latter is the Existence *(Existenz)*. Fact-of-Existing as Being-in-Time is a sort of intermediate Being, half-real, half-ideal. Or rather, it pertains to the intermediate stage between Being and the Extant. This stage manifests itself, however, as a process of concretization, as a link between the abstract and the concrete Being, and we have already seen the significance of this.

The *essentia*, the *essentiality (Wesenheit)*, the *What-ness*, are really a matter of concept formation and definition. These logical features stand in the service of the latter, and are ultimately a mode of Being. The essential is distinguished from the non-essential, the contingent. The Extant, the Being of which is this essential, is called an *entity (Wesen)*. An entity is an essentially extant being. And this is where the critical situation of Being and Extant arises.

Suchness is the essenceful *What-ness* generalized with respect to that which is essential — the quiddity. It has given up the difference between essential and non-

(*) *Translator's Note*: In German, *Da* means *here*, and *Sein* means *Being*. The word *Dasein* (literally *Here-Being* or *Hereness*) is used in ordinary conventional German as a synonym for *Existenz*.

essential, but has retained the character of *essentia*, essentiality *(Wesenheit)* and *What-ness*. This makes it a link between the essential as an abstract Being and the entity *(Wesen)* as an Extant, up to the individual trait. But it never reaches the latter; it remains on the side of the abstractly essential. Its concretization has this limit. Suchness, itself, has Being *(Sein)*, hereness *(Dasein)*, and existence *(Existenz)*, in the sense of the secondary conceptual application. The absolute position of the suchness content or of the essential content through the existence remains just a jump away. Suchness can never reach the positing of existence, it can just approach it asymptotically. The approach to concrete Being can take place solely through this "jump" of existence.

The Extant, the Being of which is the essential factor, the extant being, is the very element defined from the viewpoint of this Being as substance, substratum and material vehicle. An abstractness prevails here — one to be repealed by concretization. It is the concretization of concrete Being. It attends to that loosening up of materiality and substantiality which makes the Extant Being-ful *(seinshaft)* and overcomes the abstractness of suchness and *essentia*. But at the same time, also the *Thatness* of bare existence is filled with new content. Existentiality becomes "Being-content-fulness" *(Seinsgehaltlichkeit)*.

The *essentia* is Being, at the outset of its ways. The *existentia* is Being, at the outset of its ways. That which is non-essential is non-essential only by the gauge of concept and definition, not by that of abstract or even concrete Being.

We cannot say that the hereness *(Dasein)* of the vein *is* the suchness *(Sosein)* of the leaf, but merely that it *belongs* to it. This will be still clearer if we use the stronger expression: the existence of the vein belongs to the essence of the leaf, but is not this essence itself. And it is also wrong to say that the suchness of the leaf is the hereness of the vein; the proper way to put it is that this suchness *encompasses* the hereness of the vein, and the essence or being *(Wesen)* of the leaf encompasses the existence or Being *(Sein)* of the vein. Not hereness and suchness, not existence and essence, are correlated here, but *that which has hereness (Daseiendes)* and *that which has suchness (Soseiendes),* the existent and the extant entity. This is where Hartmann made his mistake. On the one hand, his assertions are too subtle and require a simplification. On the other hand, he makes them too easy and too simple — where he fails to see the full difference between Being and Extant, where he fails to give Being its due, where his knowledge of the essence of the transcendental is insufficient, where his transcendent realism becomes a short-circuit which impedes the opening up of the transcendental sphere. These errors must be remedied before the theory of categories can rest on a more solid foundation.

According to Hartmann, himself, the first link of the whole or this whole itself is a predominant factor of the existence. It can no longer be suchness of an Other. "The whole" is taken here as the extant world. Let us accept here this questionable concept formation. Since existence is Being, this predominance suggests that we are to leave the Extant and go over into Being, itself. Thus, not essence and existence, suchness and hereness, are made relative, but pertinence and encompassment. Existence cannot be made relative to anything — for it *is* Being.

The essentialities *(Wesenheiten)* and qualities are

external, persistent, accidental, superimposed. We have already seen the situation in this respect. The vehicle is the materially extant under the definition of the abstract Being of the concept concerned with the cognition of the essence. This does not impair the reality of the superimposed. It has a Being, a hereness and an existence, no less than the vehicle. The shortcoming of the state of externality *(Ansein)* consists in something else. It is a transcendent-realistic approach and beginning which wants to develop further. It is like a seed which wants to bud and grow. It is the existential fruit of abstract Being. The more concrete this becomes, the more thorough will be the disappearance of the difference between the vehicle and the superimposed, the more manifest will be the naivity of this foothold in thoughts of essence.

Now we come to Ideality and the Ideal. We have already gained an insight into the relationship to essence. The Ideal begins with the essence, and with the amplified essentiality *(Wesenheit)* which is suchness *(Sosein)*. But ideality is still more encompassing. It comprises not only the logical, but also the mathematical, space and time, not ony thinking, but also outlook and intuition, then the value-content based on sentiment. Even this does not yet exhaust the realm of the Ideal. There is an esthetic, a sociological, and a religious Ideal. Also where suchness, *essentia* and essentiality are present in the extant Real, they remain ideal in their Being. They can be ascribed a Being, a hereness *(Dasein)* and an existence, but this is a secondary concept formation, and this goes in general for Being, hereness and existence of the Ideal. The Extant, with ideality running through it, must be distinguished from the Being of ideality itself. Ideality is not synonymous with irreality. Ideality is timeless Being with timeless validity, but time, itself, is ideality, too. The idealities which extend beyond the essential, such as the mathematical and the values, participate in the concretization of Being. But they do not suffice for the accomplishment of the full concretization of concrete Being. The last transcendentals are the very ones to show a transcendental-realistic character, which is something entirely novel and unique; it combines the transcendent-realistic and the transcendental-idealistic, as well as ideality and reality. A certain abstract Being-likeness is retained by every ideality, concrete as it may be able to be in comparison to the prime abstract Being of essence and concept. The later ideality divests itself of the character of being a superimposed attribute. Thus, for instance, space-time is ideal Being, but no longer such an attribute. However, ideality, too, comes always short of reaching the individual element. We can regard an ideal concept, say, the number *Two,* as an individual entity, but here once again we are dealing with a secondary, non-basic and applied concept formation which cannot be lined up with the primary and the basic. Also the number *Two* is subject to the rule that of all the infinite number of contradictory pairs of predicates one will apply to it, so as to give it an all-pervading individual definition. But the negativities here become so numerous, and the positivities so small, that the value of this technique of all-pervading definition becomes questionable. Not so in the case of the true individual entities.

We shall see later how ideality is linked to subjectivity, and how, for instance, space-time, as ideality, is object-determinant subjectivity.

Existence, itself, is ideal — this is a great paradoxon. We speak of existentiality, too. The same holds true for abstract Being, while concrete Being is the advance synthesis of Real and Ideal. But reality, itself, is ideal, too.

Now we shall look at reality. Against ideality the Extant stands out as real. Reality involves Being in time, individuality, the full presence of the pre-requisites, etc. Kant says that the Real is that which corresponds to perception. The Extant is existing as the posited *What*-content, as the *That* of this positing. It is real as a oneness of *That* and *What*. Existence, as distinguished from suchness, has already passed the sudden turn to the otherness of the positedness. Reality is the growth and development of this seed. Reality is the determinator of the transcendent-realistic view of the Extant as Extant. Only concrete Being overgrows reality. Reality is a big step forward in concretization. Reality is concerned, especially, with the first definitions of the Extant, the material vehicle, the substance, the substratum. This is where it stands out most expressly, without being any less reality in other situations. This state of affairs goes so far that there is even a reality of the ideality, that which does not cancel out the ideality of the reality. Reality is ideality, but not *the Real*. This is where the difference between Being and Extant comes into its own.

Hereness and existence are moments of Being. Essence and suchness are moments of ideality. Reality and ideality are modes of Being. Essence and suchness are thus moments in a mode of Being. Now we come to the modalities of Being — possibility and impossibility, factuality *(Wirklichkeit)* and fictionality *(Unwirklichkeit)*, necessity and accidentality. Here, too, it is solely a matter of the fundamental definitions. Everything else must be reserved for later investigations. Kant characterized the modalities through their relation to the totality of cognitive capacity, as opposed to relation to the material object in general. He takes here for point of reference an expression, the choice of which is not so fortunate psychologically. But he uses it in order to express something essential, gnosiological and ontological. Just what this is, we shall see later. Hartmann wrote a special paper on the modalities, which we shall be discussing soon.

According to all the above, we can distinguish, first of all, between ideal and real possibilities. The ideal possibility includes also the logical possibility, of which consistency is the criterion — in other words, the applicability of the category of identity. From the transcendent-realistic point of view, which predominates in Hartmann's statements, the real possibility has the criterion of the completeness of the real requisites of an Extant. In this situation, that which is really possible, is at the same time also really factual *(wirklich)* and really necessary. This is its main difference from the ideal and the logical possibility. But it is merely the intermediate link to a still stronger group of modalities — possibility of Being, factuality of Being, and necessity of Being — which has other laws than those applying to real possibility, real factuality and real necessity, which are outweighed by the former ones. Hartmann overlooks this group, because he knows Being only insofar as it is the Being of the Extant as Extant, but not insofar as it differs from the Extant. Possibility, factuality and necessity of Being might mean impossibility, accidentality and contradiction for the Extant, and this possibility is overlooked by Hartmann. But this is the very aspect where the importance of Being over the Extant could become manifest. Details and whether or not it is so at all, must be deferred for later investigations. The modalities of

Being could be quite different for the concrete Being than for the Extant and the ideal which belong with it. Accidentality of Being and impossibility of Being, if there are any such at all, would then be also stronger than real impossibility and accidentality, and than impossibility and accidentality or essentiality.

The fact that factuality (*Wirklichkeit*) is more than reality becomes manifest not so much with respect to the ideal (we called the factuality of the ideal also its "reality") as to concrete Being. Its reality remains referred to the Extant, whose Being it is. But it, itself, possesses that plus of reality for which we reserve the term "factuality" (*Wirklichkeit*). In the factuality of concrete Being, reality becomes elevated to the maximal degree of its effect. Correspondingly, non-factuality (*Unwirklichkeit*) is more and stronger than the ideal. It is truly the irreal.

The original modality of existence is factuality, in the form of the factuality of the absolute position of an essential content, which we call *non-fictiveness (Faktizität)*. With respect to essences and the ideal, the logical, the mathematical, etc., the part of originality is played by possibility and necessity, as logical possibility and necessity, as mathematical possibility and necessity (on the basis of space or space-time), etc. In this connection, factuality finds here its secondary application by existence as non-fictiveness. Reality is the extension of non-fictiveness under the conditions of time, the individual factors, and of sensation (according to Kant). The development of non-fictiveness culminates in the factuality of concrete Being, which is the Being of the Being-toned Extant.

Ideal possibility is more than the logical one; real

possibility is more than the ideal one; possibility of Being is more than the real one. An analogous rule applies to the other modalities of Being.

The possibility of Being is the filling and fulfillment of all types of possibility, based on the convergence of essence and existence, hereness *(Dasein)* and suchness *(Sosein),* ideality and reality, toward the concrete Being. The other modalities show an analogous situation. Thus, the necessity of Being, in contrast to real necessity, is a necessity of a novel type, which springs forth from the progressive transcendentalization. Here it is no longer a matter of the presence of all real conditions in a structure of the Extant, so that the Extant, being really factual, is also really possible and really necessary; the point here is a necessity which is the necessity of the concrete Being itself, which is beyond the differences between suchness *(Sosein)* and hereness *(Dasein), essentia* and *existentia,* ideality and reality. Real necessity concerns an Extant which has not yet become Being-toned by having a Being which is concrete Being in this neutral sense. And this is the foundation of the plus-content of the necessity of Being over real necessity. But this can be recognized only if the trancendent-realistic view remains open for the transcendental-idealistic one and its march, which does not stop so easily. For this is just what pertains to the revelation of Being itself which makes Being *per se (Ansichsein)* a pleroma of appearance.

Now, a word more about Hartmann's "strata" which refer to the structure of the real world. They are strata of the Extant, not those of Being. They encompass the mechanical, the organical, and the psychical (and this includes, partly, also the logical and the gnosiological), and the spiritual. The investigation of the basic ontological categories changes here into a part analysis. The categories of Being experience the richest metamorphosis in their applicability. The progress through the realm of the Extant witnesses alternating ebbs and tides of categoriality. The transcendent-realistic views of sciences find here their field of activity, but also the transcendental manifests itself on an increasing scale. The general theory of categories blends into the special one. But the decision about itself is not within this realm of the Extant; it is within the scope of concrete Being itself. For the latter is the true *"per se"* of this realm of the Extant, the basic ontological problem of which cannot be decided by splitting it into appearance and thing-in-itself.

A special position is held by the category of modality of freedom. It is a second reference to the category of necessity. The latter is antithetical to accidentality and to freedom. Accidentality is the first reference. The antithesis to necessity splits, therefore, into two antitheses. This has profound ontological reasons. Thus, for instance, the freedom of concrete Being might appear in the realms of existence and reality, as accidentality; this freedom of Being might be accidentality of the Extant. This would mean the revelation of the characteristic difference of a further ontological relationship between Being and Extant, and at the same time the brightest light would be thrown on freedom and accidentality.

This would illuminate also the relationship between freedom and causality, for the latter is linked with the Extant as Extant, as against Being — and the same applies to substantiality, too. Kant viewed freedom as a causality *sui generis,* as freedom in the positive sense, to use Hartmann's term, not as freedom *from* something, but as freedom *for* something, as freedom for a moral deed. Freedom as arbitrariness of choice belongs in the category of accidentality. This is the negative freedom which tones Being down to the Extant. On the other hand, positive freedom is the freedom of concrete Being, and if we want to construe this as causality, it involves a total revolution of the causal concept, for the latter is then carried into Being, to the very extent as Being differs from the Extant. This is moral freedom, and ethics and valence acquire here their share in concrete Being. These raise the question: What is ethical Being in the light of concrete Being? We can then perhaps retain the Kantian terminology, construe freedom as causality, but indubitably we are dealing with a border-line problem, which calls for a treatment according to special laws of Being. Neither abstract Being nor the Extant of this Being is sufficient to do justice to the problem of freedom. This is the sphere in which natural and natural-scientific causality moves, so long as it does not, itself, reach its own boundary.

A good example for the freedom of abstract Being is the freedom of essentiality *(Wesenheit)* and of ideality. Concept formation has a peculiar logical freedom. Human thinking enjoys moving in it, but it must pay for it the price of substractness. The same applies to the other idealities. Thus we can even speak of a mathematical freedom, which moves in the independence of relevant individual instances. Spacetime is the immeasurable possibility of all forms, and this stretches the boundaries of the movement of mathematical freedom. But, again, this is bought for the price of such an intuitive and formalistic abstractness as the characteristic of spacetime.

Now, then, even though the realm of values is ideal, yet the situation becomes totally different in the treatment by values. This is why the ethical, the esthetical, the sociological and the religious freedoms are no longer the ideal freedom, but real one. The problem of freedom is decided here on its way to concretization, and the freedom of concrete Being in this makes an appearance, which for other spheres remains under the sign if impossibility and contradiction. We cannot go into a detailed analysis of this situation at this place.

7

THE GIVENNESS OF REAL BEING (SEIN)

The above heading is the title of Part Three of the *Grundlegung*, comprising pages 151-241. This part, too, is divided into three Sections, the first one of which is entitled *Die Erkenntnes und ihr Gegenstand* (Cognition and its Object).

Chapter 22 — Gnosiological and Ontological Being per se (Ansichsein)

The Extant does not melt into the givenness. This is its aporia. It makes now a decision for realism, but something ideal is involved, too.

The concept of Being *per se* has an epistemological background. But Being-an-Object is a Being, too. It cannot be reduced to the bare gnosiological. The gnosiological Being *per se* is a *per se* always for *me* alone. One of the two sides must be eliminated. The point is to make sure it is the right one, the one relating to the subject. This leads to the ontological Being *per se,* and this is at the same time the elimination of the reflection, the return from the *intentio obliqua* to the *intentio recta*. The eliminated element remains preserved at the same time, as taught by Hegel. Extant

74

per se and Extant *for me* are simply Extant suspended into Extant as Extant.

In the cognition, the object becomes known, not the image. The latter must be objectified by a second awareness, and this is subject to the same law. This is where reflection sets in.

Chapter 23 — *The Transcendency of the Cognitive Act*

Being *per se* cannot be proved, nor does it need any proof. We deal always solely with givenness but if it is explained as semblance, the burden of proof rests on this scepticism; it is up to this scepticism to explain the semblance. The Being of the semblance would only be another Being *per se,* without which one just cannot do.

The query for the *How* of the givenness of Being — and no other one — is the decisive question. Thus Kant, too, asked, *"How* are synthetic judgments a priori possible?" not *whether* they are possible. There can be no doubt therefore as to the *whether* as for the Being *per se* either.

Moreover, not the objects are transcendent or immanent — the acts are. They play a part not only in consciousness, as in the case of thinking, imagination and fantasy. They go beyond consciousness. The Extant is something supra-objective. Only one term of the relationship is in the consciousness. The other one assumes a position of "beyondness." It is not even necessarily extra-conscious. It may, in turn, be also a conscious act or a content of consciousness. Cognition is not *just* an act, but as an act it is a transcendent act. Cognition is misunderstood if regarded solely as thinking or judgment.

Cognition moves in many acts, in transcendent and

non-transcendent ones. But true comprehension *(Er-fassen)* is a transcendent act. It produces an image, too, which is immanent. This image, alone, can be had — the object cannot. The intentional object belongs to the immanence, to the image. In the cognition of the object that is *per se* only the subject undergoes a change, but not this image. It does not saunter over into consciousness.

Chapter 24 — *The Antinomies in the Phenomenon of Cognition*

Cognition is accidental with respect to the object. The antinomy of Being *per se* and Being-an-Object consists in the combination of correlative dependence and independence of one with respect to the other. The solution consists in the insight that Being *per se* is not identical with Being-an-Object. Being-an-Object is external to the Extant *per se,* but not vice-versa. Being *per se* is essential to the object. Every antinomy that can be solved is spurious. True antinomies have no solution.

Another antinomy is that of the transcendency of phenomena. Phenomenon *A* does not necessarily mean the Being of *A;* it can be also the Being of *B.* An example is the movement of the Sun about Earth. But does this mean that it is impossible to establish evidence of the Being *per se* of *A?* Cognition exceeds its own phenomenal character. This is something similar to — but not identical with — the transcendency of acts. Could the transcendency of phenomena, itself, not be just a phenomenon? But then the semblance would have to be explained. It is reasonable to suspect that phenomena of transcendent acts are, themselves, transcendent phenomena. At any rate, however, this can never be established directly on the phenomenon of Being *per se*. *A* appears as Extant. (In the example of the Sun and Earth, the movement of the Earth appears as the Extant instead of the movement of the Sun.) It is an essential property of the essence of the phenomenon that it transcends itself. Its content goes beyond itself. The phenomenon of Being *per se* is no exception. It makes the general relationship singularly palpable. This does not cancel out its phenomenal character.

Phenomena are unstable. They only have the Being-character *in genere*. There remains the possibility that there is no Extant *per se* in individual objects of cognition. We must guard against a prejudgment here. But a decision can be reached.

Chapter 25—*Transobjectivity and Supra-Objectivity*

Insofar as the Extant contains a non-objectified *objiciendum*, there is something transobjective standing opposite the objective. This is the problem of the unknown knowable, the expression of which is the problem awareness itself. It is an eminent Being *per se* phenomenon. According to it, the transobjective necessarily must have Being *per se* — the Being *per se* which still lies beyond the range of the subject-object correlation. This involves the Socratic knowledge of ignorance. But could the problem awareness, too, be just a phenomenon? Yet, for all that, this is the retreat of a border-line which manifests the cognitive process, and the latter gives an adverse testimony of reality. But the Being *per se* of the transobjective does not, in any way whatsoever, degrade the Being *per se* of the objective. We have already stated that the object does not saunter into the consciousness.

Chapter 26 — *The Limits of Knowability*

Nothing is intrinsically inaccessible to cognition. The Extant *per se* is defenseless against cognition. The question is only whether the congition is capable of making every Extant an object. There is such a thing as something unknowable to us. There is such a thing because of the limit of our organization. Even sensory cognition grasps merely sections of the knowable. Is this true about the conceptual, too? Our cognitive knowledge is bound to categories which are tuned to the vitally necessary. Such problems as life, freedom, psychophysical insight and prime cause, contain something unknowable to us. Principles or categories of Being are inadequate for certain categories of cognition. This includes infinity, the continuum, the substrata, individuality, the concrete totalities. This involves the most simple and the most complex. On the other hand, our cognitive organization is adequate for finiteness, discreteness, the sum total, the typical, the partial aspect. The laws of logic, too, seem to lead to such genuine and insoluble antinomies which would manifest the limit of the law of contradiction, for instance, if antagonism were contradiction.

This infinite remainder in our problematics of knowledge possesses a significant essential weight. Let us use the term *transintelligible* to denote all that lies beyond this second border-line. This boundary, too, is merely gnosioloigical; it adds nothing to Being, and detracts nothing from it. Neither is the eternally unknowable non-extant, nor is it the Extant proper.

The irrational has Being *per se,* for the object as a whole is homogeneous. If a part of it is relative to the subject, so is all the rest of it. If a part is extant *per se,* so is also the entire object. For the movement of the border-line does not produce any change in Being. The elasticity of the border-line thus becomes a significant evidence of reality. The process of becoming an object does not de-power the Being-character of the Extant.

Section Two — The Emotional-Transcendent Acts
Chapter 27 — Emotional Receptive Acts

While cognition is the more transparent act, at the same time it is also the weaker and secondary one. It is the only non-emotional act. The emotional acts bear a tinge of activity, struggle, energy, daring, suffering, personal concern. They live in the dealings with persons and in the doings with things. They are the acts of experiencing, endeavor, craving, doing, acting, wanting. They relate to a success, a failure, an adverse experience, expectation, hoping, apprehension. An answer as to value itself is emotional act-toned. The border-lines blur, sharp types can only do harm. The feature common with the act of cognitive comprehension consists in the transcendency of the act, the Being *per se* of the material object, the conviction of the Being *per se* of the world. The category of reality shifts completely into the foreground.

Our next topic is the class of the emotional-receptive acts. They have a different act structure than that observed in cognition, which leaves the physical object unaffected. This group includes experiencing, noting, adverse experience, the necessity of tolerating — in general, adversity. A blow, a push, pain, teach a drastic lesson on the givenness of reality, without causal conclusion and without reflection.

Adversity signifies the state of being at the mercy of the solidity of the Real. Cognition follows later. Examples: The experience of a deceitful person, or the revelling in the consequences of one's own action. Escape is confined between narrow limits. Observation is no aim here. I can direct attention, but not adversity itself. It overtakes me as an act of fate. This is an eminent certainty of the Extant *per se.* Cognition and understanding do not go hand in hand. "Experiencing" in this sense is not "intellectual grasping," but being grasped, being unnerved, being seized, being overcome.

Chapter 28 — Gradation of Experiencing and the Unity of Reality

We become aware of the material reality by experiencing resistance. This is the conscious awareness of impeded activity. It relates to the heaviness of a stone no less than, for example, to the might of the prevailing law. It is a drastic evidence of reality. The motor sense and the sense of touch play a predominant part in the certainty of reality. This is what Scheler chose for the foundation of his voluntative realism.

Things are not merely objects of awareness, but also objects of craving, struggle, barter, purchase, etc. They involve material and spiritual Being. The latter is non-spatial, but it is Becoming process, once-ness, duration, sequence, simultaneity. Real time plays the decisive part for both types of Being.

In living and dealing with people, theoretic cognition plays mostly no part at all. The attitude is the primary thing; the object-subject relationship is secondary.

Chapter 29 — The Emotional-Prospective Acts

Man has foresight. He expects that which is in the offing. He assumes an attitude of acceptance and an acquiescent readiness toward it. He stands before the incalculable, the unsuspected, the surprising. He anticipates. These, too, are transcendent acts, and they are broader than the corresponding cognitive ones. Expectation, presentiment, readiness, resignation, are based on a drifting with the temporal current. Man is not ahead of himself (as Heidegger asserts), but merely reaches ahead of the present with his consciousness. That which approaches has a tremendous weight of reality. Expectation, presentiment and readiness are not cognition. Yet these attitudes are fallible. Something else may occur, too. This contingency is also in account. Man counts on uncertainty itself. He makes his arrangements, seeks protection and flexible adjustment. All this is a strong evidence of reality. A secondary form of this presentiment is curiosity, with its inquisitiveness and thirst for sensation. It is the will to be surprised.

Chapter 30 — *True Emotional Acts of a Prospective Nature*

These include hope, anticipated joy, fear, and anxiety. The new feature here is the selective emphasis on value. The valuable and the disvaluable are results of selective judgment. A mood of optimism or pessimism develops. The accopanying feeling of impotence against the oppressive becomes an overpowering testimonial of reality.

A peculiar phenomenon is the reliance on the "lucky break." This is often linked with the false metaphysics which seems to teach that hope is a merit and a desert and will get its reward. Man fools himself with this. This includes games of chance and gambling on the stock exchange, and if things go bad, the gambler attempts to force chance, and he even works out "systems." This is the illusory element in pre-concern and the borderline of the transcendency of the act. It develops into the disposition to see things through rose-colored glasses, or into the tendency to see everything black. The illusion loses contact with the Extant *per se*. This is a phenomenon similar to fantasy in the theoretical realm, an emancipation from real happening. But fantasy still has the innocence of play.

Anxiety offers most frequently an opportunity for false anticipation. It destroys the calm reckoning with the Real. There are self-tormenting metaphysicists. Fanatics exploit the fear of death. It is an evil thing to take oneself too seriously. If death is nothing but annihilation, there is no evil. Man gains succor here in viewing himself as a drop in the stream of universal happenings. Respect for the great, combined with modesty, brings freedom from the metaphysical legerdemain of anxiety. Unbridled self-tormenting is immoral. Heidegger's analysis of anxiety (taking the fear of death for its model) followed the most tragical and most consummate of all self-tormentors, Soeren Kierkegaard. This blocks the way of return to the *intentio recta*. This way of thinking makes itself incapable of a dispassionate look into the Extant.

Chapter 31 — *Emotional Spontaneous Acts*

Now we come to dealing with the true activities— with desiring, wanting, doing, and acting. They are founded on an active anticipative manipulation of the future. This is the very miracle of human nature. Man can no longer change the past, but he can change his present — and hence, the future. Anticipation holds a special kind of transcendence. Something real is produced; a delusion is possible here, too, but a tendency to realization cannot be denied. This is more than the Being of the purpose in man's consciousness.

An indirect receptivity is linked with the direct spontaneity. The resistance of the matter must be overcome, and this is attempted again and again, in new approaches, in *work*.

Secondly, the individual is *retroactively affected* by his own act. This is a real force, no less real than an external one. Man is blessed and cursed by his action. He perceives a sense of responsibility for it, which overcomes him suddenly with an overwhelming force.

Thirdly, there is a "reality-weight" of persons for persons. This encompasses more than is taught by utilitarianistic ethics, the mere external *consequences* of the act. The existential weight of persons for persons is greater than that of things and matters. But one must not ascribe the character of reality to persons while denying it to objects, as some of us do. Reality is no existential privilege reserved for entities.

Chapter 32 — *Inner Activity and Freedom*

This is where the specific character of interpersonal interlinkage manifests itself. Acts of moral disposition, such as benevolence and jealousy, sympathy and respect, reverence and contempt, hatred and love, are all directed at a material object. But where they concern an abstract, like in "love of gold," or "love of one's country," persons become involved. This is where the reality-givenness finds an expression. Primary givenness shows itself also in the assumption of basic attitudes, as in revulsion and attraction, in "opening up" and withdrawing, in nearness to or distance from individuals.

There belongs here, furthermore, the rôle played

by the situation and its form of givenness. It comes uninvited and compels to action. It is a state of duress, but not without a certain latitude, a compulsion to freedom. Man is forced to make a decision. This is why responsibility and guilt appear. Every decision in a value-conflict encompasses the danger of becoming guilty. This is, however, a definite testimonial of reality.

Section III — Real Life and Cognition of Reality
Chapter 33 — The Scheme of Life as Extant

Actions combine into patterns. The stream of consciousness and the stream of world events show a penetrating transcendency which does not vanish anywhere. The sum total of the act transcendency is the real *modus* of life.

The value sense answers to the Real, not to that which is merely a product of the imagination or of the thinking process. This is the weight of reality in the value-references.

The material world shows a practical givenness. In utilitarian objects, the *Being-for-us* is more important than the Being *per se*. Heidegger called this *Zuhandenheit* — meaning *availability* (literally, "being at hand" or "at-handedness"). "Hereness of something for us" would be a more descriptive expression. But also the Being-for-me is a Being *per se*. It has its reality weight. The tool remains the Extant *per se* (providing that I do not alter it or improve on it), but *I* improve in making use of it. Heidegger's analysis is valuable; it has disclosed a primary mode of givenness of the Real. However, he makes the mistake of confusing it with a mode of Being. And thus the world is the "ever-mine." Availability already has a Being *per se*-character. The revealedness of the world is a strict givenness of reality.

Heidegger speaks of "concern" *(Sorge)*. This is a teleological prospective act. The valuable in it is the reconstruction of a consciousness as primitive as possible. However, it remains an open question whether this can actually be done. "Concern" is but one manner of a large group, which includes wanting, endeavor, action, doing, expectation, fear, hoping. The ontological yield of the analysis of "concern" is slight.

Chapter 34 — Special Spheres of the Footing in the Real World

These include, first of all, the real phenomenon of Work. Its resistance must be continually gauged on the topic itself. This has its moral aspect, such as the application of force. It is never without a reference linkage to persons. Its reality weight is the ontological aspect of the phenomenon of work.

Further real interrelations show new forms of givenness. They include the contact and dealing with human beings in the social, legal, political and historical vital interrelationship as the field of phenomena of overall situations Their movement constitutes History. The overall situation does not tell man *what* he has to do, but it leaves margin for his decision. It used to be right to have slaves, today it is wrong. Capitalism and Communism propound different doctrines concerning property. But not only the whole affects the individual, but also the individual affects the whole. There is a definite testimonial for reality in all this.

A further rôle is played by life in its relationship to the cosmic scheme. We are part and parcel of an orderly course of Nature. Summers and winters come and go. At times, Nature overthrows everything, as in earthquakes, floods, etc. How small and helpless man appears then! Such might impresses him as the Hand of Fate. But superstition seizes on this, to speak of an intervention of the gods, of a Tribunal of Judgment, etc.

Chapter 35 — Cognition and Emotional Givenness

Does the emotional benefit or hamper the cognition? There is only one real world which shows segments of the given. There are differences between the world known through personal experience and the world revealed by intellectual cognition. The overlapping must not be exaggerated. Visual and tactile perceptions, for instance, are not so far from each other as claimed by some modern psychologists. There are no purely visually perceived things. They are an offspring of psychological reflection.

Thus, certain conclusions follow from the transcendence of the emotional acts. The emotional evidence of reality remains referred to comprehension. Only the theories achieve an artificial unfolding of comprehension, which is then as if floating free in the air. This may seem to be a meager epistemological result, but we are dealing with ontology.

Further consequences are: Perception is embedded in the emotional life scheme. This is both a strength and a weakness. The same applies also to higher cognition. The situation is somewhat different with respect to science, but science too, remains bound to life. It shows a retroactive foundation on the scheme of life. Cognition has the advantage of objectivity, of the comprehensive view, etc., but also the drawback of a lesser certainty of reality. Therefore, it requires complementation. Its weight falls on the side of suchness (*Sosein*). But with reference to the hereness (*Dasein*) of the world, the complementation takes place through the mode of

Being affected. The emotional-transcendent acts carry a certainty of the reality in the world as a whole.

Starting with the *a priori* elements of cognition, the kind of givenness of the phenomenon transcendence tapers off gradually, to the emotional-receptive acts.

Chapter 36 — The Special Status of Cognition

Cognition is secondary to life. The border-lines between the two are blurred. Cognition cannot be isolated. There is a homogeneity and an antithesis in the act interrelationship of the two. In cognition, emotionality peels off, the state of being affected vanishes, but only within the framework of this interelationship.

Also first-hand knowledge, experiencing and adverse experience have their suchness *(Sosein)*. It is always definite. The same applies also to wanting, action and doing. Only cognition introduces the difference between suchness-givenness *(Soseinsgegebenheit)* and hereness-givenness *(Daseinsgegebenheit)* into the multiformity of acts. Hope and fear show a certain blurredness and unclarity. This is the other aspect. All we have to do is observe the way in which we frequently become aware of a scene in the street.

Cognition practices criticism and scrutiny. It is, as it were, a judge among the positive acts. But this involves the threat of an overemphasis on science, and the development of an intellectual prejudice. A certain emancipation of science leads to its estrangement from reality. It becomes pragmatism, mere utilitarianism. The formulas are no longer adjusted to the phenomena, but the phenomena to the formulas.

But the way in which Bergson and Husserl criticize science fails its purpose, too. They combat, with full justification, an empty science, but to the benefit of a mere synthetic *naïveté*. The phenomenon is merely a starting point, a plane of attack, a surface. The act phenomenon is not an object phenomenon by far as yet.

Chapter 37 — *The Position of Science*

Various methodical errors and misunderstandings are involved here. The embedment of science in the life scheme must not be overlooked. The homogeneity of the belonging to one real world is nothing less than the fundamental law of the givenness of reality. There is an acute need for the correctness of scientific-critical prejudices. Exact science is never purely quantitative. Symbols like *m. t. g. v,* represent relationships of quanta — substrata and dimensions. This reveals the analysis of concepts such as body, forces, energies, real process, event, affecting and being affected. Rules are always those of a Real. Laws and relations are not only *in mente*. Laws are automatically real laws. They are subject to error. Science is not isolation, but a synthetic view. Theory means "viewing." Science is interested in the whole. But the gift of conspective view is rare, and this affects science adversely. Only a few are the chosen ones. As regards this synopsis, philosophy remains the conscience of science.

Cognition has an ontological footing. The emotional-transcendent acts have the tendency to result in cognition. Every philosophy of the mere Ego-reference is based on a gross misunderstanding. The world is not somebody's world, for that somebody already stands in a world in a real fashion. The world is the stage and the common plane of Being of every possible correlation. Ontologically, "I and the world" and "I and my world" are just as wrong as "God and the world." Either does God exist, and in that case He is part of the sum total of the Existent, the real world — or He does not exist, in which case He is no contrast to the world. The same applies to the Ego. The "world" category is to be assumed, from the very outset to be the all-embracing one.

8

THE CERTAINTY OF REALITY

The neutral attitude which Hartmann believes to be assuming at the beginning, is no true neutrality. It stays by no means "on this side" of idealism and realism. His point of view is, beforehand, a disguised realism. His endorsement of realism only serves to bring the one-sidedness of his approach to light. Yet, he is not entirely lacking in transcendentalism. His Ideal is a transcendental temperance of his Transcendent, but its interpretation follows the pattern of the transcendent-realistic view. It persists in this secondarily applied concept formation, and does not permit the attainment of that transcendental view of the Ideal which alone is adequate for it and lends expression to the entire Transcendental.

We are dealing with a quaternity: Being *per se,* Being an Object, Being a Given, and Being for Me. The state of being an object is a property of the extant appearance (as distinguished from the essential phenomenon; but this expression is applied to the extant appearance, too) and it has a *"Being* per se *for me"* — a highly paradoxical concept. The Being *per se,* insofar as it is more than being an object, is the genuine Being *per se* which attains to its fulfillment in concrete Being. But this concept goes always hand in hand with a second label — the *"Being-toned Extant."* Both are needed, together, for denoting what is truly meant. We shall see later that this circumstance attains to its great significance, for instance, in the ontological motivation of the philosophy of religion. Both concrete Being and the Being-toned Extant can only be represented in the simile of an extant contradiction and of an existential impossibility by the Extant *per se*, and this circumstance has transcendental reasons. However, the state of being given, being an object and being for me has developed and attained to fruition in both. It is revealed as Being which gains the upper hand over the first realistic Being *per se* and fulfills it. It reveals the depths of Being *per se* of the Extant *per se*. This, and only this, is the entire phenomenon.

Transcendent-realistically, however, the Extant does not melt into being an object and givenness. But transcendentally, the deeper moment of Being lies just in these plus the *Being for me*. This is where these three cease being something epistemologically and ontologically inferior in value. However, also these border-lines — being an object, being given, and being for me — will be crossed in the deeper and more remote regions of the transcendental, but this will not be concerning us for quite a while yet. But this effects a *still further* transcendentalization of the transcendent-realistic element, this time in the sense of a transcendental realism. In this connection, the main issue is not the termination of the state or reflection, but — on the contrary — its fulfillment. But this presupposes the complete passage through all states of reflection, which describes a circle and leads back to the original lack of reflection.

Hartmann says that in the relationship of Being *per se* and *being for me* the object side must be reduced

— in other words, the *being for me* into the Being *per se*. But the Being *per se* must be absorbed also into the *being for me,* as soon as it becomes obvious what transcendental moments of Being are contained in *being for me.* This absorption will then occur quite automatically, and this is just what results in the self-revelation of the Being *per se.* To be sure, this is still not the ultimate, but it leads toward it. *Being for me* is also Being *per se,* only different from the former. The Being of the subject is encompassed, too, and put in the service of revealing the objective material Being *per se.* This is the genesis of concrete Being and of the Being-toned Extant. True, the extant subject cannot be made the fundamental definition, but the Being of the subject mediates betewen Being *per se* and concrete Being. The definition of Hegel, stating that the eliminated factor is preserved, suffers from the shortcoming of taking the Extant as Extant for the determinant. In Being, the sides are, rather, mutually intertwined, becoming something totally different.

If Extant *per se,* object, given and *Extant for me* are merged into Extant as Extant, the evil of substantialization and all that is connected with it can never be overcome.

It is impossible to imagine a relationship of two terms, one of which is in consciousness while the other one is outside of it. This is a violation of the law of homogeneity. The basic epistemological problem expresses itself in this aporia and antinomy. There is absolutely no conceivable relationship to the Extant *per se.* It stands outside of every relationship. Let it remain an open question here whether there exists an unthinkable, totally irrational and transintelligible relationship. You can conceive of such a thing, but not by thinking of a relationship, but of something extant, construed in secondarily applied concept formation on the analogy of a transcendentally extant object. The relationship existing simultaneously within and outside of consciousness is not this relationship. It belongs much rather to that which is appearance, that does possess the full solidity of reality, too, which makes it independent from conscious awareness. And there exists also a relationship to this that-which-is-appearance, one term of which exists within consciousness and the other outside of it — not, however, in the sense of genuine Being *per se,* but in the sense of the phenomenal trait of the extant appearance. This must not be mistaken and misconstrued, but must be kept clearly distinct. That-which-is-appearance is saturated with immanence and picturesqueness. It is totally in the conscious awareness and totally outside of it at the same time. This cannot be said about the thing-in-itself, and this is the very factor that presses toward the manifestation of concrete Being and of the Beingfully Extant. The position of the fundamental problem is thus far more precarious here than Hartmann believes. It contains a turmoil which finds its peace in Being only. In comparison with this, the contrast to the mere thought content, figment of imagination and product of fantasy is secondarily and empirically psychological. That-which-is-appearance is always simultaneously also *like* — but not *merely* — some figment of thought and imagination. It is fully intentional object and fully non-intentional object. This is a dialectical relationship. But this does not apply to the thing in-itself, the inconsistency and impossibility of which points at Being itself. The contrast between appearance and thing-in-itself compels to a deeper exploration than is carried out by Hartmann. And it is true that that which cannot be proven is concrete Being itself — true existence. It is the only basis for the proof and demonstration of the Extant *per se* and of that-which-is-appearance. It is the manifestation of the latter. Being itself, is comprehended in an original belief, the structure of which is a peculiar one.

That-which-is-appearance is pervaded by a semblance, but Being is the antithesis of semblance. Yet, Being makes a visible appearance in the Extant. In that-which-is-appearance, the semblance is a reference to Being, Herbart's statement, "As much semblance, so much Being," holds true here. Mere thought, imagination and fantasy produces another semblance, which is *nothing but* semblance, and which is not to be mistaken for the semblance of appearance, which is the Being-semblance — as sunlight and the mirage are two entirely different types of light phenomena.

Pure and full Being is the source of all evidence, the true beginning and the true end. It is that by which everything is proved, that which therefore cannot be proven, itself. It is the *That* of existence. It can be demonstrated how Being solves the problems of the Extant. This is where the *How* lies — also the *How* in Kant's question, "How are synthetic judgments *a priori* possible?"

A transcending act is a contradiction to itself. No act can transcend. If it did, it would cease being an act. The movement of the act toward that-which-is-appearance is no true transcendence. It is the paradoxical *Being* per se *for me*. This fact was already recognized by Hegel. The transcendent-realistic beginning of reflection must take this contradiction in account, too. But it is there in order to be nullified, which happens through the unveiling of the transcendental. *Being* per se *for me* becomes a deeper, fundamental stratum of Being. The objecthood of that-which-is-appearance is intentional and non-intentional at the same time. The equilibrium is reached in the view of Being *versus* the Extant. Being is act fulfillment and act nullification. In the act, Being was implied. Being is transcendence itself, the immanence which remains transcendent.

If an act or content of consciousness is made an object, this is a secondary concept formation on the basis of reflection. It remains dependent on the model of materiality. This situation is simple and devoid of problems. The fundamental problem has vanished. The point now is merely that this immanent objecthood shares in the blessings of that which has become of the transcendent objecthood, which overcomes materiality. This reinforces then the line of the transcendental which lies so naturally close to the act and content of consciousness.

Indubitably, cognition is misconstrued if evaluated only as thinking or judgment. Empirically, cognition is thinking plus intuition *(Anschauung)*. Ontologically, it belongs to Being, and Being gives cognition its plus as compared to thinking. But since also thinking belongs to Being, there is a very interesting concrete difference in this plus.

It is true that the material object does not saunter over into consciousne, but something of it does get over. We can express this also inversely by saying that consciousness with its cognitive limit advances into the material object. These are symbolical expressions, in terms of movement, borrowed from spatial terminology, and the relativity of the direction has no real meaning here at all. It is just as if we were saying about time that it moves from the past toward the future, or from the

future toward the past. Actually, there is no real movement involved. The correlative dependence of the sub-
ject-reference of the object is turned by the transcendental into an independence stronger than the independence of the first Being *per se*. Something about the transcendent becomes contentualized. The transcendental is
the continuation of this contentualization on the transcendent itself. Hence, objecthood is not external and
accidental to Being *per se*, but is essential to it. The
externality, indifference and accidentality of Being *per
se* with reference to the objecthood applies only to the
first transcendent-realistic approach. That which is a
true antinomy for the latter, can be solved in the transcendental. It is therefore not true, as Hartmann believes, that every true antinomy is insolvable. He only
reaches this conclusion because he regards the transcendent-realistic as the fundamental, decisive factor.
The solution of the antinomies is based on the very fact
that the transcendental outweighs the trancendent-realistic.

The comparison with the weight-mass relationship is
inexact. Mass shows independence, weight shows dependence. To this extent, the comparison with the relationship of Being *per se* and objecthood stands. But the
difference is that weight remains relative and never becomes the Being predominant over mass, as it is the case
in the relationship now under consideration. The analogy fails here, because it has been drawn entirely from
empirical experience, whereas the relationship in question involves the transcendental.

In Hartmann's treatise, the antinomy of Being *per se*
and objecthood is followed by the antinomy of phenomenon transcendence. Once again an empirical example
is used to elucidate it — the movement of the Sun and

Earth. Phenomenon *A* does not need the Being of *A;* it may mean also the Being of *B.* Something that is transcendentally extant, exists factually, only the *What* and the *How* are questionable. The movement of the Sun is replaced by the movement of the Earth. The phenomenon transcendence remains unaffected. This simile, too, says little about the problem itself, for the transcendence of the movement of the Sun and the Earth is that of something-that-is-appearance. But in the case of the phenomenon transcendence, the transcendence of true Being *per se* is the point. In the sense of intentionality, every phenomenon trancends itself. The true epistemological-ontological query has not come up at all as yet with respect to the transcendence of that-which-is-appearance. Empirical phenomena, such as the movement of the Sun and the Earth, fall back in their problematism, not by one but by two degrees. The question whether the Earth or the Sun is in motion no longer involves the *"per se*-for me" character of that-which-is-appearance, but that entirely different something which both possibly moving objects are *per se* in the metaphysical sense. This is the start of the march toward pure Being. This problem of phenomenon transcendence is one degree nearer to the transcendental than is the problem of act transcendence. This is the difference between the two. The Being *per se* of the Extant *per se* is itself a phenomenon, but one of a special nature. The Extant *per se* cannot be directly observed. It is taken for granted, it is always already unveiled, and is the prime requisite of the possibility of every cognition. The phenomenon of transcendent Being *per se* is, in fact a transcendent phenomenon. With respect to it, the theory of Being is the most reasonable belief. Reason and belief coincide here. The Extant *per se* is the great Opposite to all intentional objects. It has no intentional object of its own. This is its distinctive feature. It can be observed only through the coherence of concrete Being. The Being-character *in genere* is Being itself. The abolition of the oblivion of Being is not based on an arbitrary metaphysical prejudgment, but on the prime *a priori* itself.

The still unknown, the problem awareness, the cognitive process, the knowledge of ignorance, are a testimonial of reality for that-which-is-appearance. The notion that a cognitive limit is advancing, as it were, into the Extant and rips off a part of its unknownness, is — as we have seen — a totally inept idea. It is much more important to see how the advancing cognition unveils the Extant *per se* by demonstrating the trancendental and thereby reshapes the transcendent-realistic foundation of that inept notion.

The transintelligible or irrational is the real representative of genuine Being *per se,* of the thing-in-itself, of the ever unknowable. This is the very instance where that-which-is-appearance is transcended. This is where Being wants to manifest itself in connection with a process of concretization. The irrational-transintelligible Extant is revealed by the transcendental, which summarizes itself in Being. The transcendental question begins where transcendent-realistic query must end because no more is possible — and new answers become possible, eventually even leading to an ultimate transcendental realism, which is neither transcendental idealism nor transcendent realism. This is where the ontological motivation of the concept of God becomes possible. Ontology supplies a religious-philosophical approach.

If the unknown knowable has Being *per se,* so has that which is known, and vice-versa. If both have Being *per se,* so must have the ever unknowable, too, only in the increasing sense that the former *have* Being *per se,* but the latter *is* Being *per se* — namely, as Being. It is Being *per se* by its nature, it is identified with *Being per se,* it is Being *per se* itself. This is where the problem of the transcendental emerges. This is something totally different from a sauntering of the object over into the subject. Transcendent realistically, the Extant-in-itself is defenseless against cognition, but not transcendentally, for here cognition is a part of Being *per se,* its Being is also Being *per se.* Cognition cannot make an object out of every Extant. The Being of cognition will be exceeded in manifold ways later.

Our sensory cognition deals only with segments of the "Extant which-is-appearance," and this is the case also with higher cognition. This is an empirical limit of our organization. But this discreteness is compressed in Being, itself, into a continuum, and gaps are filled. The cognition of the Extant is tuned to the practical vital necessities, but the practical is just what has not the least understanding for Being and lives in deepest oblivion of Being. Heidegger calls this the *"Man."* Theoretical reflection knows full well that our cognition exists for something more than for the practical vital necessities. It has to become quite impractical, and this benefits practice ultimately, too. We might even be working, through the very *intentio obliqua,* on a reorganization of our organization, to make it more and more Being-toned, and thus to bring it nearer to its ultimate goal. In that case, the theoretical would have an eminently practical significance. This would give our biological organization a far greater variability than it now possesses, and thus a greater adaptability, as this difference already exists between the animal and the human being. But this could have its sequel.

Now as for the logical laws, a distinction must be made between the laws of formal and ideal logic, on the one hand, and the laws of real logic, on the other hand. This is where the problem of the extant contradiction and existential impossibility comes into view. That which is really conflicting is not contrary to the law of contradiction, as Kant demonstrated in his criticism of Leibniz — for the very reason that it is an appearance. Quite other problems are the ones here in which the extant contradiction and the existential impossibility become acute.

It is not true that the second border-line, that of irrationality, adds nothing to Being and detracts nothing from it. Irrationality is not purely gnosiological, but ontological, too. The separation of the two is feasible abstractly only, and only if the transcendent-realistic becomes a prejudice. Eternal unknowability has another relationship to Being than the temporary one. It is an essentially other Being *per se*. Every that-which-is-appearance is open to cognition. The transcendent thing-in-itself is eternally inaccessible to cognition as Extant (it cannot even appear in our thoughts — one can only *believe* in it) and this is the very thing that becomes accessible to cognition through Being itself. This does not mean that it is necessarily impossible for Being not to belong to the cognition of the knowable unknown and of the known, too. But that is the becoming acute of the epistemological-ontological fundamental problem. Infinite residues are residues of the Extant. Being is no residue. It makes the irrational residue the reservatory for the extant residue and for that of which it is a residue.

It is an amateurish attempt at conceiving of the Extant to assume that the homogeneity of the total object consists in that if a part of it is Extant-in-itself, so is the other part and the whole, too. This separation into part and whole does not exist in Being. Being shows the true homogeneity, out of which the true specification and manifoldness become manifest. Becoming an object does not de-power the Being-character, because it manifests the Being, the absolute empowering which cannot be de-powered. After all has been said, we can again speak of the Extant as Extant, in the sense of the Extant become Being-toned. It is beyond the antithesis of Being and Extant, of appearance and thing-in-itself, of the subjective and the objective, of the transcendent and the transcendental, of ideal and real, of essence and existence. It is a new approach and outset for a last part of ontology. But then we shall no longer speak of the Extant as Extant the way Hartmann does, but in an entirely different manner. Being has attained its goal in it, and so has everything transcendental and all reflection. A circle has closed. It is a return to something original, simple, naive, to something that is more than *intentio recta*. It is the Extant pure and simple which the subject lets be Extant pure and simple. The description of objectivity in this ultimate is the highest achievement of ontology.

Now we come to the emotional-transcendent acts, discussed in Section Two. Here, Hartmann presents a great deal of empirical-psychological details. His analysis is distinguished by fineness and a wealth of wit. But Hartmann stops where ontological query proper should begin. His main mistake is that he fails to distinguish between the practical certainty of reality, which is theoretically worthless, and its theoretical counterpart. Kant saw deeper here, and Hartmann does not know his Kant well enough. The difference between the thoretical and the practical with reference to the certainty of reality was an extremely serious problem for the great man of Königsberg. We could also call this the "transition problem." The question was how the transition could be effected from the realm of Nature to the realm of mores, and vice-versa. Kant penetrated deep here. He saw that practical reason displays its own peculiar reality awareness which, however, leads to no decision in favor of theoretical reality awareness. The difference runs parallel with the regulative and the constitutive. One of the Kantian formulas of solution was that entire Nature finally becomes a symbol for the realm of mores — but this represented just one side. Kant thus created room for a moral belief. But this still did not solve the purely theoretical problem of the certainty of reality. Hartmann's mistake is that his emotional-transcendent acts are, in a naive-realistic fashion, a direct theoretical testimonial of reality — which simply vaults over all the Kantian efforts of thought. This way of proving reality sounds of what the logician calls *argumentum ad baculum*. It cannot overcome any scepsis or convince any sceptic. Every sceptic admits to the practical conviction of reality induced by a blow, by an impact, or by pain, without letting it sway him in his theoretical doubt of reality. A great deal of what Hartmann says would show up well in an empirical anthropology. The only trouble is that it has nothing to do with the epistemological-ontogical fundamental problem. The view of the prime *a priori* is missed. It is not sufficient to render an indubitable testimony of reality for that-which-is appearance, as Hartmann does. This does not comply with the requirements of the problem of Being *per se*. These are the three mistakes which are interlinked: 1) The overlooking of the fact that the emotional-transcendent acts produce only a practical certainty of reality; 2) that the latter only refers to that-which-is-appearance, possess as it may all the solidity of reality; 3) that the transcendental and the ideal are imaged transcendent-realistic-materially, that which unveils its own characteristic mode of Being. The comparison with Hartmann demonstrates what a profound transcendental thinker Kant was.

The essential character of knowledge is not based on its being transparent but also weak, secondary and embedded — its essential feature is that it writes the formal constitution of the epistemological-ontological fundamental problem of Being *per se*. It is only from this point on that also the emotional-trancendent acts, with their purely practical transcendence, may contribute something to this constitution. They follow cognition along its path through all the reflection of the *intentio obliqua*. Cognition sets the first example and leads the way. Concrete Being reveals itself, the one in which the transition problem becomes settled. Now the practical-regulative can be made useful for the theoretical-constitutive. Finally, the Extant reveals itself anew as the Extant. Now also the embedment of cognition can be seen in the proper manner. Its embedment in a vital interrelationship of purely practical import is still not the right one. The Extant become Being-toned is, in its entirety, the prime *a priori*. Thus the non-emotional element, the cognition, is used for putting the emotional to a constructive service. This is still far from done by the practical conviction of the Being *per se* of the world.

Modern phenomenology, represented by Husserl, Heidegger, Scheler and others, has recognized anew the significance of the practical, the pre-predicative, the naïve, and the natural. But it has resisted the temptation to regard the practical testimony of reality as a sufficient satisfaction of theoretical conscience. It has set out on the quest for the prime *a priori,* and in this undertaking it has had to apply genuinely transcendental methods. Heidegger set a shining example here. He did not skip over the Kantian transition problem.

It is part and parcel of the difference of reality from existence, hereness *(Dasein),* essence and ideality, that reality — which relates to the temporal, individual, processual, to genesis and perishing, and to history — contains, next to the theoretical-constitutive moment, also a strongly practical, pragmatical-regulative moment. This leads to a vast unfolding of the reality category, as soon as this practical moment can be made useful to the constitution of Being *per se* — what, however, cannot be the case directly. Only so will the transition take place from the practical act transcendence (where not only the act but also the transcendence is of a non-theoretical and practical character) to a theoretical act transcendence, which now embraces also the emotional. This is the diffcult problem of theoretical reality, which then stands out so richly and typically against hereness *(Dasein),* existence, essence and the ideal.

If I go too near to the stove, the heat makes me feel pain. The pain knows nothing of a theoretical Being *per se.* If I am far enough from the stove, I experience the sensory perception of warmth,* which through reflection can factually expand into a theoretical knowledge. But in the first case, an artificial act of reflection must be superimposed on the practical one in order to bring about a theory, and this is not identical with the one mentioned, but is a theory of sensory data. The transcendent-realistic object function is used as a model

---

* Berkeley has used this example.

which compels to the introduction of a law of variation, in which this object function reshapes itself plastically. This is how the practical *per se* differs from the theoretical one. Unlike adverse experience, cognition can enter the immeasurable transcendental, which must first be opened up for adverse experience. The practical conviction of the Extant *per se*, produced by the blow, the impact and the pain, is instinctive and drastic. It needs no causal conclusion, no reflection. But it is only when reflection follows that the practical conviction is theoretized, that the passage into the transcendental is opened up, that access is gained to the theoretical problem of the *per se* which transcends that-which-is-appearance.

The retroactive affectedness by my own acts and the development of the sense of guilt about them is no purely practical matter. My own doing becomes a real force through the presence of this state, from which realistic effects issue forth to act upon me, as though from an external force. They produce a theoretical cognition which precedes the practical one here. The retroactive effect becomes retroactive affectedness. I become compelled to direct my attention and my reflection onto the retroactive and retro-affective factor. This is how I begin to emerge from the prison of the mere fatalistic view.

A certainty of reality may have great practical force and yet be theoretically weak. The practical strength is no substitute for the theoretic prevalence of truth. It is frequently so with the state of being concerned, shaken, overwhelmed and overawed. Genuine theoretical comprehension is like a tender voice deep within the spirit, which testifies to truth. Being seized is just what can drown out this sound. Once upon a time, The Lord revealed Himself to Elijah not in the raging of the tempest, not in the earthquake, not in the thunder

and lightning of the storm, but in a soft and gentle rust-
ling. Elijah covered his head and worshipped The Lord.

The experience of resistence through a stone is different from that gained through the power of the existing law. The latter has only a secondary and symbolical
materiality and stands much nearer to the transcendental. The same may occur in the case of the stone, but
only through advanced natural science — as though we
no longer saw the stone with the eyes of a child, but with
the eyes of an Eddington. But in that case, the entire
experience of resistence has been transcendentalized.

It is to be feared that also Scheler's "voluntative
realism" fails to do full justice to the Kantian transition
problem.

Real time holds a practical element in addition to
the theoretical one. We can call it "practical time" and
can contrast it with theoretical time. This imposes a
highly significant task on the time analysis. This problem
must be treated in an interrelationship of Being and
Time.

If in the course of dealing with people one mostly
never even gets to know people, one sees where the interest of the practical *does not* lie. What is to be expected
here for the epistemological-ontological fundamental
problem, the most theoretical of all problems? Practical
conduct is not interested in the true *per se*. It has not
even the sight for it, and it does not suspect that just
this theoretical question is of an eminent practical significance. It is as though you asked a stolid shoemaker
to prove Einstein's theory of relativity.

Now we come to the emotional-prospective acts. In
anticipation, we must also distinguish between the theoretical and the practical. The former is moved by Being

and wielded by science, the latter by the Extant and has an emotional character. The scientist works in a symphony of observation, query by experiment, and a creative divination on the basis of the most profound ties to Nature. Understanding of Nature is always opened up for him beforehand. Hence, it is possible for him to master the Extant, to dissolve entire realms of relationships into relationships of laws, which manifest themselves as the Being of the corresponding extant realm. The practical man, on the other hand, insofar as he is no more than that, sets himself against what is in the offing, assumes a defensive position, adapts himself, etc. He is moved by the Extant, in its full mysteriousness, and he has no inkling of the Being and Being *per se* of what seems to be approaching him, what incides upon him out of the future and is thus the "incidental." Temporality, with its three modes, already strongly bears the mark of a transcendental; it is a stipulative condition, an object-stipulating subjectivity and ideality. Subjectivity is not identical with the extant subject; it is the Being of the subject, which is Being *per se* at the same time. Temporality is an arouser of attention, alertness and reflection; this is a part and parcel of its essential nature. This ends mere practice; this is view, *theoria*. There exists therefore a difference between the theoretical and practical pre-sentiment and anticipation of man. Only the theoretical one merits the name "foresight," for it *is* fore-sight.

Hartmann says that man only reaches forward with his conscious awareness, but he is not ahead of himself as Heidegger teaches. Once again, Hartmann fails fully to understand Heidegger. From the purely anthropological point of view, Hartmann is right. But that which

Heidegger says is something inaccessible to empirical anthropology. He unveils something of the prime *a priori*.

At any rate, uncertainty and deceptivity are taken into account in practical expectation. Uncertainty can be eliminated only by the incipient theoretical cognition, which is a continual definition in anticipaton, too. And even deceptibility is defined and measured by cognition.

The practical attitude can seal itself off against cognition, in which case the will to delusion and illusion comes into being. Anticipatory cognition, which precedes will like a torch-bearer, can teach us what to choose when under the influence of hope and fear. The practical is blind without the theoretical. The latter is the eye of the practical.

It is bad enough when the contact with the Extant *per se* is lost through a premature closing of the transcendent-realistic knowledge. It is even worse when the same loss occurs with respect to the concrete Being. In that case, a sceptical or dogmatic delusion with respect to the Being *per se* sprouts forth. Such scepticism is itself dogmatic, and this dogmatism always leads again to scepticism.

Hartmann now proceeds to discuss *dread (Angst)*. Once again he misunderstands Heidegger. In his opinion, Heidegger followed Soeren Kierkegaard, most tragical and most consummate of all self-tormentors. Self-tormenting metaphysicists and religious fanatics exploit man's dread of death. They take themselves too seriously. If death is nothing but an end, there is no need to dread it. Man ought to see himself as a drop in the stream of the scheme of cosmic happenings and ought to stand in awe before the Great, and to exercise humility. Let it remain an open question here whether these naturalistic advices are sufficient really to help man in his dread. There certainly exists an immorality of unbridled self-tormenting, but whether this formula does justice to the great phenomenon of Kierkegaard may be justly doubted. It is to be wished that Hartmann had possessed more of the penetrating trancendental insight of Kierkegaard. Heidegger did not hesitate to learn from him—and he benefited by it. Heidegger regards dread as a readiness for freedom chosen by man himself in awakening from the oblivion of Being of the *"Man"* to true revelation and resolution. It is of an ontological character; it reveals something of the prime *a priori* of Being itself, and is therefore totally different from the fear which is directed at *something,* whereas dread concerns the *Nothing,* as which Being itself appears to the Extant, insofar as Being is the foundation and background of the Extant. The Being of dread is therefore Being-for-death. But this is the very point where the finiteness of man becomes active, the finiteness through which he, ahead of himself, returns to himself. Precious glimpses into the depths of the transcendental, these! This is why the other side of this ontological waking and awakening dread is courage, bravery, the discarding of cowardice before dread, the fear of dread, joy, security and appeasement of eternal yearning. This is how man becomes the keeper of Being. Hartmann completely overlooks the structure of this analysis. He understands Heidegger superficially only.

In evidence, let us exhibit a few quotations from Heidegger. Let us select for this purpose the small (forty-seven pages) but significant and meaty paper entitled, *Was ist Metaphysik?* (What is Metaphysics?), published in 1949.

"Dread manifests the Nothing" (p. 29). . . . "It is in the Being of the Extant that the Nothing manifests its Nothing-character" (p. 32) . . . "More abysmal than the mere suitability of thinking, negation is the solidity of active opposition and the sharpness of abhorrence. More responsible is the pain of failure and the ruthlessness of prohibition. Heavier is the acerbity of deprivation" (p. 34) . . . "The dread of the hazzardous tolerates no contrasting to joy, or even to the comfortable pleasure of calm living. It stands, on this side of the boundary line of such contrasts, in a secret alliance with the serenity and mellowness of creative yearning" (p. 32) . . . "Hereness *(Dasein)* means being held into the Nothing" (p. 32) . . . "The miracle of all miracles: *That* is extant, That which is called, in its essence, into the truth of Being, is therefore always tuned in an essential fashion. The clear courage for essential dread guarantees the cryptic possibility of the experience of Being. For awe *(Scheu)* dwells in the vicinity of the essential dread *(Angst)* as the terror of the abyss, Awe *(Scheu)* clears and incloses that side of humanness within which man remains at ease in the enduring."

These quotations ought to be sufficient. They show that no attempt is made to escape dread and to suppress it by naturalistic deliberations of a questionable character (well known to be a futile undertaking), but it shows a way into Being, which is a real way of escape. Ultimately, the certainty of reality is founded on a pure belief which is not even able as yet to tag the great mystery of the factual *(das Wirkliche)* with such labels as "Being" and "Extant," but whose expression is "Nothing," in a totally new and concrete sense. This is the very spot where the spring of the true certainty of reality proper gushes forth. This is no scepticism and no doubt, but its diagonal opposite — belief. This Nothing points at that which no longer lies as "Being" and "Extant," between subject and object and is possible content of conscious awareness, but at that which, as fullness itself, is inexpressible, that which is actually meant by "Being" and "Extant," that which is the source of the meaning of the latter. But we have touched here upon something that belongs not to a criticism of Hartmann but to a criticism of Heidegger. We cannot follow it up here.

Now we come to the emotional-spontaneous acts. Something future is brought forth in a real fashion, after a purpose has been set in the conscious awareness. In the realization, a transcendence occurs. But again, this is practical transcendence, and its relationship to the theoretical transcendence problem calls for a specific treatment.

There are three things to be distinguished. Things, persons, and one's own act and person exercise their effects. The light and shadow of the practical and of the theoretical are differently distributed. The work overcomes the resistance of the matter. In this case, as in that of retroactive affectedness by persons and by oneself, we are already dealing with syntheses of the practical and theoretical. Two quite different transcendencies coincide, of which only one — the theoretical one, the certainty of reality — runs beyond that-which-is-appearance. The practical transcendence is introduced here into a higher context, over which it possesses no power. It plays a rôle purely with respect to the non-phenomenal Being *per se*. It goes toward Being and its concrete Nothing.

Man often experiences the power of the Other to close itself before him, more strongly than the power of things. But then he lives completely in practical transcendence. The metamorphosis to the theoretical involves a reduction, and this is a good thing, too. It brings him an alleviation of this bitter situation.

Now we get to Section Three. The broader, more encompassing vital relationships are considered here. In this connection, Hartmann speaks of Heidegger's analysis of "accessibility" (Zuhandenheit). He regards it only as a curtain-raiser which must not be overlooked. Heidegger's "ever-mine" world must not be understood purely subjectively. The subject is at his world, to start with. He does not confuse a mode of givenness with a mode of Being; the former is, itself, a mode of Being.

In Heidegger's terminology, "concern" (Sorge) means primarily "care" (Besorgen). It is applied to utensils (tools). The Latin word is cura. The other meaning, as shown by the conclusion of Part Two of Goethe's Faust, is not totally absent; it is also present as an overtone. The main aim is not even the unveiling of a most primitive consciousness. Concern is the basic structure of hereness (Dasein). It has, properly speaking, two modes — care (Besorgen) and solicitude (Fürsorgen). Heidegger significantly correlates this analysis with the relationship of Being and Time.

Cognition is embedded in the matrix of vital interrelationships and must not be isolated. But the embedment in an Extant is inadequate for the essential nature of cognition. The mode of Being affected is primarily a practical one. Cognition is in the Being, which is capable of becoming the concrete Nothing of the belief in the certainty of reality. This meets the requirements of the theoretical nature of cognition. The emotional has the stronger certainty of reality, which is *of another kind* — of the practical one.

Cognition is by no means bare of every emotionality

and affectedness. The scientist takes an ardent interest in truth. This may involve the most powerful emotions. A certain part of science interprets Nature as akin to mathematics. This and other elements need by no means become an intellectual prejudice. The clarity, transparency and the criticism of cognition bring freedom from the blurredness of purely emotional objects, without degenerating into cold, totally emotionless intellectualism. The latter sets in only where cognition is misused. The viewing of concrete Being and of concrete Nothing is a protection against it. But the intuitionism of a Bergson, to be sure, is no remedy against it. He did not see the full Being and the purity which is the concrete Nothing of the belief in reality, but saw only an empirical form of the time-bound view. Husserl really discovered things of the prime *a priori,* but he lapsed into intellectualism far more than Heidegger and Scheler.

This is what Hartmann says about the God problem: Either does God exist, in which case He is a part of the sum total of the Existent, of the real world — or He does not exist, in which case He is not a contrast to the world. Hartmann displays no interest, in all his writings, in the religious-philosophical problem, but solely in the ethical one. According to him, the world category must be understood *a priori* as the collective, all-embracing one. This is where the transcendent-realistic limitation of Hartmann becomes evident. The sum total of the Existent and real world is constructed entirely on the pattern of the transcendent thing. The religious-philosophical problem is just what forces one, according to the realistic side, into the same direction as idealism — to entering the transcendental. But this moves the world category as an all-embracing concept into the salubrious criticism of the Extant as Extant. The sociological problem itself is already a prelude to the religious-philosophical one in this essentially ontological respect. The concrete Being and the concrete Nothing have a word to say about the antithesis of God and World, of God and Ego, of Ego and World — a word which is no longer audible in Hartmann's view. He lacks the very means of expression for it. This is the consequence of basing ontology on the Extant as Extant. This kind of Aristotelianism is *passé*. It already began to be passé in the teachings of pre-Aristotelianism. In this respect, Aristotle already represents a degeneration from the understanding his forerunners had of Being. We must not try to turn back the wheel of history. It would be a futile attempt. The road runs from the Extant to Being, and over the latter to the true reality consciousness.

9

THE PROBLEM AND POSITION OF IDEAL BEING

This is the fourth and final part of the *Grundlegung* (pp. 242-322). This part, too, is divided into three Sections. The first Section is entitled, *Die Gegebenheit des mathematischen Seins* (The Giveness of Mathematical Being).

Chapter 38 — *The Ontological Aporia of Ideality*

Does ideality only indicate possible Being, but has no Being itself? The *a priori* concerns only the How, not the *That*. Is there at all an ideal Being and an ideal cognition? These questions manifest a fundamental aporia and its consequences.

The ideal is unobtrusive and was discovered late. It involves no state of being affected. It prevails quietly and concealed. It does not overwhelm us as an act of fate.

The inducement for assuming here a givenness of Being is supplied, primarily, by mathematical knowledge. The Pythagoreans were the discoverers. For instance, the statement that the symbol π equals $3.14159\ldots$ expresses a fact, not an idea.

But a triangle exists only *in abstracto*, as a triangle

115

per se. The mathematical concept of a triangle has only an intentional object. But the geometrical judgments are silent about this. They deal with genuine objects. The inverse mistake is that of regarding the mathematical as unideal and purely real. *Three* would then mean three things, from which the Three is abstracted. But this is a wrong theory.

Mathematical judgment is clearly distinguished from the mathematical object. The concept of the polygon, itself, for example, has no angles, but the polygon has. The referend is the polygon *in genere.* In ideal Being, concept and referend are easily mistaken for each other. Truth and untruth are referred to a polygon itself.

Mathematical Being therefore posesses Being *per se,* supra-objecthood, independence from becoming or not becoming known. It does not originate in the judgment — as neither do the real things originate in the judgment.

Chapter 39 — Theories and Views

Modern axiomatic research has furthered a mathematical subjectivism. Here everything depends on the first positings in judgments. The rest is then solely a matter of a conclusion according to the law of contradiction. The Eleventh Axiom of Euclid, the axiom of parallelism, is a good example of modern axiomatic criticism. It has led to other geometries.

A second outlook is mathematical intuitionism. It makes the mistake of taking the postulating act of intuition, and not the given object, for basis. In this case, though, everything is based not on prime positings, but on prime evidences. Objects are only intentional.

This leads to fatal consequences. Everything is contained in conscious awareness only — the positing thinking as well as the postulating intuition. The latter is a little nearer to factuality *(Wirklichkeit)*. The fundamental epistemological mistake here is that *having* a content is not tantamount to *comprehending* an object. The former state is immanent, the latter one is transcendent. Phenomenology reacted against it, but then suffered, itself, a reversal. Husserl was converted to idealism.

But mathematics without cognition is then meaningless, because it is objectless. It is then merely a glorified chess game played according to certain rules of thinking.

Chapter 40 — Ideal Cognition and Objective Validity

There is an immanent and a transcendent *a-priorism*. The intersubjective generality of the *a priori* is the harmony of subject with subject. This is not sufficient. A harmony of the subject with the object is needed. But how can we find out whether this is actually attained? This is where the characteristic cited by Kant, the moment of necessity, is helpful. Plato's "mathematical boy" is a good example.

It was a great idea of Plato that mutual contact, as brought to expression in the dialogue, compels the state of affairs to show itself. Thus, ideal *a-priorism* and necessity, necessity of thought and necessity of Being, seemed to be interlined. But this, too, is still insufficient. The Cartesian doubt does not vanish, the *deus malignus* would still be possible.

Chapter 41 — Ideal Cognition and Real Cognition

The great miracle now is the full applicability of mathematical cognition to real conditions. This is how the Pythagoreans already saw it. The mathematical principles of knowledge are at the same time the principles of the things themselves. This led to exact science, but also to an irresponsible numerological mysticism. The ideal is only potentially real, but the real is pervaded through and through by the ideal. It must therefore be more than subjective, especially if we consider also the power of the emotional for the certainty of reality.

The astronomer forecasts eclipses on the basis of his calculations, and the predicted eclipses will occur. This is more than a mere-cause-and-effect relationship of acts, of conscious awareness or of thinking. Nature would not follow the dictates of these. This is a genuine self-revelation. Mere chess-game rules of thought are not adequate or sufficient here.

An equivocation in the concept of ideality becomes a drawback here. "Idea" means, on the one hand, a mere notion, a fantasy, an act-borne intentionality, something immanent, something *merely* irreal — or, on the other hand, it is a mode of Being *sui generis,* an independent givenness. Nature is *per se* mathematical. The ideal neither is mere mental imagery nor does it fuse into the Real, but it asserts its own mode of Being against the latter.

Section Two — Interlinkage of Ideal and Real Being
Chapter 42 — The Disappearance of the Ideal Objects in the Field of Cognition

The concept lies before the ideal. Why do the concepts not press into the foreground this way in the case of things, too? This happens only in artificial theories, as in subjective idealism and in Neo-Kantianism. On the other hand, in the case of ideal Being, it occurs quite naturally. It is hard to distinguish the concept (or intuitive perception) of the triangle from the triangle itself.

The conceptual is here in the foreground and performs an act of repression. This is why a conceptual existence seems to be involved, especially since the emotional falls out.

The object has an importunity and an inobtrusiveness. Pure spacial and magnitudinal relations remain submerged in the Extant. When brought forth, they assume a logical structure. This is feasible without a confusion of identities only where the real relationships are taken in consideration.

The cognitive complex has a definite position in ideal cognition. Unreflected cognition perceives the object through ideation, but without being aware of the latter. Such awareness is first awakened by reflection. Science then goes the way from ideation to concept. But the mere ideation is identical with the image.

We must distinguish between two disappearances. One alternative is that the image or the ideational representation disappears, and the object presses into the foreground. This is the case with naïve apperception. The other alternative is that the image presses into the foreground, and the object disappears. This occurs in mathematical and ideal Being. Different modes of Being are linked successively behind each other.

Chapter 43 — The Threefold Successive Linkage

Ideal Being assumes a position of proximity to consciousness. It is an intermediate position at the same time. It is perceived in introspection. A special reflection, an intuition, is needed to discover it. Thus, there is a position of proximity and remoteness with respect to consciousness, an intimacy with consciousness, and a strangeness to consciousness. Ideal Being is distinguished by these. Our consciousness is not equipped for noticing ideal Being; it stands too close to it. Thus, we arrive even at a threefold successive linkage: the image, the Ideal, and the real object. This is too much for our consciousness. It exceeds its strength. The ideal object vanishes, at times into the image, at times into the real object.

This also explains many a thing involved in the medieval battle between nominalism and realism. The *essentia* slips away either into the concept or into the things or into divine beyondness. In the third case, the real Extant is degraded to semblance, and ideal Being alone is the true one then. Here even the Real disappears into the Ideal.

Even when the delusions are unmasked, they still continue to delude, like the appearance of a stick which appears broken when held under the surface of the water. You may be aware of the illusion, but that does not prevent it from affecting your perception again. Delusion is different from error. The latter vanishes when it is unmasked. This is why ontology must fight a continual battle against the delusions.

Chapter 44 — Relative Independence of Ideal Being

The Kantian moment of necessity is reinforced by that of generality. It shows a genuine independence from individual instances; it is not a collective assertion, but a really universal one.

But the true independence of the ideal object must be distinguished from its false isolation. It cannot be torn out of the context of the Real, in which the heterogeneous remains bound. Mathematical empirism is on the wrong path. For example, if *"Three"* is abstracted from only tree things, it possesses no true universality and weight of necessity. Yet, the ideal is not a second world next to the first one, no repetition, no reduplication of the world.

Ideal Being is indifferent to the real one, but not vice-versa. The Ideal is a foundation of the Real. There are idealities which never become real — such as the imaginary numbers and the non-Euclidian spaces. And yet, they have their own specific mode of Being; they are not mere thoughts, but true objects. The difference between pure and applied mathematics is a testimony for ideal Being.

From the viewpoint of the Ideal, the Real is accidental, but this is only an accidentality of essential nature, and no real accidentality. A similar argument applies to possibility and to necessity. The Ideal seems to be a realm of possibility, but only in the sense of ideal or essential possibility, not in that of real possibility. The Ideal is not the higher, but the lower, imperfect Being. The Real alone is individual, the Ideal is only general. The general is only a structural element in the individual.

Chapter 45 — *Indifference and Lack of Freedom*

The real instances are considered "inexact." No real triangle coincides with the mathematical one. Phenomena of fall and throw never obey exactly the mathematical laws. But the reason of this is not that real Being is inferior and ideal Being is perfect, but that the Real is complex. Cognition begins with an *a-prioristic* view, applies it to the Real, and in doing so it encounters the complexity. It is, therefore, quite wrong to speak of an inexactitude of the Real.

The indifference of ideal Being toward the real one has its limit here: it must never become a chorism.

(*Chorism* means severance, as opposed to distinction.)

Section Three — The Ideal Being in the Real
Chapter 46 — The Phenomenology of the Essentialities (Wesenheiten)

Husserl's method of bracketing (the epistemological reduction) and raising before the bracket (de-bracketing) is more than abstraction. It is *Wesensschau* — intuition of essence. Otherwise, it could not lead to laws of essence. It renders testimony of the ideal Being, which is neither identical with the Real nor is identical with mere ideation, thinking or cognitive perception. This leads Husserl to the discovery of the neutral suchness *(Sosein)*, and thus, indirectly, of the ideal Being. Namely, mathematical Being is not the only ideal Being. Other varieties are: the essentialities *(Wesenheiten)* and the values.

Husserl's *Wesenheiten* are genuine *universalia*. In this connection, we must distingush between a free and an attached ideality. Mathematical ideality is free, and this is what led Plato to chorism. The *Wesenheiten* are attached — not in the sense of arbitrary abstractions, but in the sense of essential structures.

The positive view thus testifies for a factually Extant *per se*. Thus, for example, the relationship of the whole and the part can be demonstrated on the terrestrial globe, on a crystal, etc., and can be taken, in a clear intuition of essence, as the common feature.

Chapter 47 — Intuition of Essence and Evidence

Descartes and Leibniz introduced the idea of a universal mathematics *(Mathesis universalis)*. It would be possible *per se,* but it is frustrated by our knowledge. It already works, in a disguise, with the idea of an *intellectus infinitus.*

The indifference of the Ideal to objectification and to the reality of the cases is a proof, in its aggregate, of the Being *per se* of the Ideal. In this connection, the phenomenological view of evidence is not necessarily absolutely reliable. It is stigmatic, not conspective. It could be conspective, and if so, it would furnish a better certainty, but this stage has not yet been reached in phenomenology. The researchers follow very divergent paths and arrive at totally different results. They are more right in that which they affirm than in that which they deny. The situation is better in mathematics, for mathematics uses the conspective view.

We must be on our guard against an equivocation between subjective and objective evidence. We have the former, but it does not help us — the latter we have not, for the criterion (which can be given, at best, as a relative one) is missing. Otherwise, the possibility of a delusion would have to be denied, and the intuition of essence would have to be credited with an infallibility which it does not possess. It would be a different story if its objects were merely intentional.

Now then, this is the positive sense of "evidence delusion"; the very possibility of error proves the Being *per se* of the Ideal.

Chapter 48 — *The Realm of Logic and its Laws*

The laws of logic are not laws of thought. Mistakes about this point are commonly made. Laws of logic are much rather ontological laws of Being. Thinking is a psychological process and is subject to quite other real laws. The laws of association supply a good example. They are only indirectly laws of thought. Logic deals with the most general thought contents, not with the psychological process of thinking. General thought contents are like mathematical idealities — free, not attached. Mathematical Being is entirely pervaded by logical Being The fact that our thinking goes by it, is outwardly something that concerns our thinking, but not vice-versa.

Thus the attached Being of the essentialities *(Wesenheiten)* is also completely pervaded by the more general logical Being, as — for example — it can be demonstrated in the law of contradiction. Therefore, the latter must be an ideal law of Being, and so it goes with everything logical.

Stronger reasons are supplied by the relationship of laws of logic and the system of real laws. Mathematical Being and the essentialities *(Wesenheiten)* already carry logical Being into the Real, but it can also be demonstrated directly. Every logical application to something real is a subscription in the logical sense, and is represented by formally proper syllogisms. The logical in the common structure of the Real and of Thought is an essential structure to both. Mere laws of thinking could be no *perceptive* thinking.

The objective validity of the logical, and of the possibility of the real sciences based on it, is the miracle of cognition. This goes so far that it has been assumed that the relationship must be inverted, in the sense that the Real adopts itself to the cognition. While this seems, at first glance, to be a simplification, it leads later to absurdities. Kant steered clear of these. He taught the adequacy of Nature to our cognitive capacity.

Chapter 49 — The Realm of Values and their Mode of Being

The values occupy a special position among the essentialities *(Wesenheiten).* The Real adapts itself to the mathematical and to the essentialities, but not to the values. This is the difference. The keeping of a promise remains a value, even if the promise is not kept. But that which then occurs in the Real, is disvaluable. However, this does not affect the Being, itself, of value. It points at an own Being *per se* of the value. The independence of the value is higher than that of the essentialities, but both are ideal.

For this reason, the Being of value has a certain "elasticity." Values are indifferent to the Real, and the Real is indifferent to the values. The value-answer and the value-reaction respond to the Real, not to fiction. For this reason, they become especially strong when, for example, a person is unfairly treated in my presense.

The value-sense is not an apperception of the value, but a state of being affected by the value. If my will scorns the value, it gets into conflict with my value-sense and is condemned by the voice of my conscience. The values, themselves, can be brought out as an ideal sphere. Thus, from the reality of a value-sense there follows the determinative power of the values — through the intermediary of the realizing will.

The value awareness changes, but not the Being of the values. Courage, fairness remain as values, but their validity as values can be different. This depends also on historical conditions. Man is characterized by a certain narrowness of value-awareness. He cannot well comprehend all values in an epoch; he is actually "value-blind" to some. Every value affects the whole man — this is why man is unable to grasp all values alike. By high-lighting values, he may become one-sided and value-fanatic.

The moments of ideal Being *per se* in general, there-fore, are: It is a process of being experienced, and the independence therefrom. It is a state of being contained in the Real, and the independence therefrom. It is indifferent to value-awareness, and to the real instances. The lack of the value-sense is not a delusion, as the lack of cognition is no error.

Chapter 50 — Modes of Being and the Stratification of Spheres

Beside the indifference of the Ideal to reality and irreality, there is also an indifferrence of the Real to a certain Ideal. The categories of the Real are not auto-matically identical with the categories of the Ideal.

The "elasticity" of the sphere is neither detachedness nor reduplication. A twofold extension takes place: the Ideal extends beyond the Real, for instance, in the plurality of mathematical spaces, and in the irreality of possessing a plurality of values. The Real extends be-yond the Ideal, for instance, in the alogical, in the dis-valuable, in the real antinomies.

Every real is individual, a once-and-only, and cannot ever be brought back. Every ideal is general, recurrent, eternal. The exclusion of the individual is the reverse side of the Platonic eternality. This applies even to the idea of the individual (as to the idea *"Caesar,"* as devel-oped by Leibniz) which is no individual idea. Thus, also the essentialities *(Wesenheiten)* of processes are, them-selves, no processes.

Th Ideal has thus been surrounded with a false halo of loftiness. The truth is that the ideal Being is the lower Being — thin, tenuous, insubstantial. That which is truly valuable is found in the ephemeral Real.

Chapter 51 — Proximity to Awareness and Ideal Transcendence

The transcendence is not cancelled between the Ideal and the awareness thereof — merely the distance is reduced. Intrinsic givenness must not be confused with immanence.

There exists an irrational in the realm of ideal Being, too. It has its problem awareness and its cognitive progress. Mathematically irrational is, for example, the ratio of a side of a square to the diagonal. If it is denoted by symbols, it is only a notional concept; if it is expressed as an approximate value, the latter is always inexact. The law of the approximate value shows a transintelligibility. The awareness-proximity of the Ideal is no curtailment of the transcendence.

"The law of identity states the identity of the different— A_1 equals A_2 (otherwise it would be empty tautology and logically meaningless) — in other words, the identity of the non-identical. It is, therefore, a law which includes the contradiction. But the law of contradiction repeals contradiction. Thus, both statements cannot co-exist; if A is non-A, it is not A — and vice-versa. Therefore, they can exist neither with nor without each other. This is against the law of the excluded middle. Consequently, the latter cannot co-exist with those two. Nor can it exist, however, without them. And this is again contradictory to its own principle." (p. 321)

"The fundamental laws of logic are, *per se*, not merely alogical, but — since the forms of intellection, which alone is suitable, are the logical ones also transintelligible." (p. 322)

10

THE TRANSITION TO MEONTOLOGY

We apperceive factuality *(Wirklichkeit)* in a faith
which is the fountainhead of all certainty. The category
of factuality is the most advanced one for the comprehension of that which is truly meant here, which is a
great mystery. But even this category is insufficient, as
also the term "Faith" is unsatisfactory for the medium
of comprehension. We use this term only because we
have no other one, and because we must use some term.
The object of faith, the content of belief, is itself absolutely inaccessible, it cannot enter our thoughts. It has
left Being and the Extant behind itself. Being becomes
negative in it; it has become something like a concrete
Nothing of the strongest impressive force, and this dis-
tinguishes it from the empty, abstract Nothing. We
might say that this Nothing is for us like a Being-like-
Non-Being, which in truth is the Being-All, the fullness,
the abundance, the *pleroma*. But even this is just an
approximative expression of the truth under the conditions of the object-subject relationship, which have
been absorbed and no longer obtain here. We just cannot get out of our skins. We cannot even state that this
belief-content is and exists, that it is the Real. If we

speak about it as the Ideal and the Essence, we have advanced still farther into the immanence which is subject to the conditions of notional representation. Therefore, we cannot even predicate the "Being" of the belief-content. There still lingers here a last residue of subjectivity which has a disturbing effect. Being here becomes actually something like a Nothing; it becomes a total else-ness even of pure Being. We are deeply affected by the feeling, the awareness, the certainty of this else-ness. We face it perturbed, shaken, unnerved, shocked to the core of our very roots, and this is an emotionality, compared to which the emotional transcendent acts described by Hartmann are mere trifles. It is in this very state of shock and unnerving that we experience the true certainty of reality. This Nothing is instrumental in giving far more insight and knowledge than is anything else. About this Nothing we could say what Faust tells Mephistopheles: "In thy Nothing do I hope to find the All."

For the annihilating and clearing element within this Belief content is not the *No* of scepsis and agnosticism — for the very reason, if for no other, that faith or belief is the very antithesis of doubt and scepticism. To be sure, it is a knowledge of ignorance, but in the sense of the *docta ignorantia,* ignorant knowledge and learned ignorance. It is not true that, as Hartmann assumes, the Ego is surrounded by a corona of the known and of the knowable unknown, beyond which there stretches the realm of the unknowable, the irrational and the transintelligible. Rather, the latter executes a motion which is ignored in Hartmann's views: the unknowable, the irrational and transintelligible advances against the Ego, seizes the spheres of the knowable unknown and the known, assimilates them to itself, draws them into itself, leaves nothing over. Then comes the last testimony that the Ego can render of truth and factuality (*Wirklichkeit*): Everything becomes the belief-content, which is so thoroughly and absolutely irrational that I can no longer even speak of its having a Being, that there simply must be something else here that I am no longer capable of expressing. But this is how I learn about truth and factuality. This does not in the least prevent the existence of both regions — the known and the knowable unknown; it is only that now I know what relative significance they have as mere approximate values for that which is truly meant — the True and Factual, the inutterable great mystery which I cannot doubt in the slightest, that is for me a source and fountainhead of all knowledge, all safety and all certainty. I revere this mystery. It instills in me fear and reverence, love and trust, dread, fright and obedience, which keep me in a continual state of sensory renewal, practically and theoretically at the same time. It brings the sacred, the awe, truth and factuality into my life. Its Nothing-character gives my life a character of purity. Now I know about the true sense of negativity, refusal, non-action, the *No* and the *Nothing,* logically and alogically, as suppression and as decision. Before the great mystery, a shaking of the head becomes meaningful. It is like a wink that demonstrates the inexpressible, that speaks the unspeakable. This concrete Nothing is the cloak of fullness; purity brings riches. It is a pleromatic purity and a meontological fullness. I find the most profound peace in it. As *pleroma,* the concrete Nothing is the *concretissimum*.

This mental disposition tends to become habitual. It is the precious prudence of the philosopher, the firmness of the soul, equanimity and serenity. It holds the strength for victory. It gives freedom from superstition and disbelief.

The great mystery is the miracle of miracles, the true freedom. The *deus malignus* remains excluded, because he is an extant monstrosity. Let us use the term *meontologic* to designate the ontological character of the belief-content, as distinguished from Being and from ontology, for Being here becomes Being-like-Non-Being, the total elseness of Being, the concrete Nothing. We can say then that if ontology is to be able to fulfill its task, it must ultimately become meontology, and this is the decisive step beyond Hartmann. Only so does ontology show its highest and strongest power of disclosure, illumination, clarification and revelation. Revelation, itself, employs ontology. Openness turns into deepest concealment. The eternal concealment itself advances into the limelight of revelation. This is synthesis, synopsis, conspection, in the highest sense. It is the spiritual law of truth itself.

Here the entire epistemological situation becomes eschatological. If we may express it naively — there must come the time when even the very belief-content is no longer something merely "believed" in the total elseness of Being, but something contentually known, whatever may become of that. The boundaries of our organization will have expanded and gained fulfillment. Subjectivity will no longer bar us contentually from the True and the Factual *(Wirkliches)*. There will be no more irrationality. We can think of this only as of a miracle. Yet, we have not the necessary ideational forms of representation, or that which takes their place. But this eschatology is in our blood. We know all about it, but we do not know what we are doing as we say this.

Now let us define our position to the individual

points of Hartmann, first of all to mathematical Being. Kant was the great pioneer here. He based mathematical Being not on thinking, but on the intuitive view, not on the empirical but on the *a priori,* not on the analytical but on the synthetical, not on the transcendent but on the transcendental. Thus he saw it as object-stipulating intuitive subjectivism of an ideal-objective and experience-widening effect. This was a mighty advance into truth. He was on the way to the insight that this concrete ideality is part and parcel of Being and Being *per se,* itself, as contrasted with the Extant and the Extant *per se.* This is exactly what makes ideality ideality. Hartmann adopts many a thing from these results. He recognizes clearly that the place of mathematical Being is on the side of ideality. It is more than the indicator of possible Being; it is inobtrusive, silently obtaining and concealed, close to awareness, but free from any shrinking in transcendence. But what Hartmann fails to see is the difference between Being and the Extant. Mathematical Being remains for him an Extant patterned on trancendent-realistic materiality which is totally immersed in phenomenality and cannot emerge out of it. He overlooks the tendency to Being and Nothing, and therefore his view cannot become sufficiently conspective. Its superobjectivity is not of the extant kind.

Mathematical subjectivism is bound to be wrong if this term refers only to the extant subject. This produces the purely methodical "universe of discourse" which starts out from axioms and effects a syllogistic construction according to the law of contradiction. This may suffice for purely mathematical purposes, but it is no objective interpretation of mathematical Being. Hartmann is perfectly right in this. But subjectivism in the Kantian sense is something entirely different. Kant does not mean the extant subject, but the subjectivity as Being and part and parcel of Being and Being *per se,* so that there results an object stipulating *a-prioristic* subjectivism which possesses a higher and better objectivity than that of material things. Hartmann fails to give sufficient consideration to this possibility. Something similar applies to intuitionism. The final and ultimate formula is neither the statement that something is contained in awareness, nor that it is outside of awareness. The same applies to the immanent subject-subject *a-priorism* and to the trancendent subject-object *a-priorism*. The ontology of Being and meontology step in everywhere and carry on what has been begun. But the result is astonishing. We have seen that the purely methodical universe of discourse, which makes mathematics a higher chess game played according to the rules of thought, is no satisfactory ontological interpretation of Being. But this methodism may, amazingly, be recognized again to be the right (as it is the case with certain quantum theorists in their debate with Einstein), if the critical meontological fundamental attitude is combined with it. Einstein believed to be able to recognize true physical reality. Certain opponents of his, including Jeans, however, knew that Einstein was mistaking mere working hypotheses for a cognition of the reality extant *per se*. This awareness is very close to that which we call belief-content as a mode of apperception of the *concretissimum* in meontological awareness. And to this extent, that which is present here is by no means scepsis, agnosticism, mere methodism, relativism, pragmatism, subjectivism, but an optimal testimony of reality in a genuine critical attitude. This has no longer anything in common with a chess game.

The two Kantian moments of universality and necessity in the theory of mathematical Being are correctly introduced by Hartmann. They ward off mathematical empirism which imagines itself to be able to abstract the ideal structures of things, and they evidence the true *a priori*. From here on, the way leads through discussion and mental contemplation, which is dialectical, to the unveiling, the removal of the disguise, which is the decisive phase of the reality problem. Meontologic belief, too, has its intentionality. Its intentional object is the belief-content, as the irrational factual *(Wirkliches)*, the unknowable referend. It is never "merely" an intentional object; it is reality itself. It is no longer an object in the proper sense of the word. This is the crux of the criticism of all intentionality. Its position is similar to that of the emotional. We have found that the latter makes an appearance, in its full primordial force, in the meontological awareness in particular. But this happens so that the weighty transition problem no longer represents a stumbling block in the way of a solution with respect to the practical and the theoretical, but the solution has appeared. The profound shock in the fact of the unknown Real, as the practical, is also the theoretical testimony of reality. And the fact that here we have something before which even the predication of pure Being proves inadequate and becomes a mere sign of the total elseness of its self, makes a mighty contribution to the solution of the transition problem, which Kant could not manage and which Hartmann fails to consider and to see sufficiently.

Nature as such is mathematical, for the mathematical is part and parcel of the Being *per se* of Nature. The question that arises here is whether Hartmann does justice to what is customarily referred to as Kant's Copernican conversion. Cognition adjusts itself to the

134

object, but the object also adjusts itself to the cognition. The mind adapts itself to Nature, but Nature, too, adapts itself to the mind. The first term of both statements holds true according to Kant, insofar as the empirical realism obtains; the second term holds true under the sign of transcendental idealism. Hartmann says that Kant emphasizes the adaptation of Nature to our cognition. But here his Copernican epistemological conversion is not done full justice, although he is right in claiming that Neo-Kantianism has gone too far in its interpretation and has become one-sided. The reason is that Neo-Kantianism had eyes for the abstract Being alone, and failed fully to recognize the concrete one. On the other hand, Hartmann views Kant too much in the realistic aspect of his system and fails sufficiently to evaluate the true meaning of his transcendental idealism. That which makes it possible to calculate and forecast solar eclipses, is itself made a part and parcel of the structure of Nature. This is a true self-manifestation in Heidegger's sense, and this is why also Nature adapts itself to the knowledge. At the same time, transcendent realism must assert the opposite, and within its own field it is right. Nothing adapts itself to the idea — which is nothing more than a notional representation, act-borne intentionality, a pure immanent — and the idea must adapt itself to everything. But there is something that adapts itself to the Ideal, which is Being and Being *per se*. The equivocation is thus cleared up.

To be sure, Being remains burdened with a trait of abstractness. This vanishes only in the negation of Being, in which an Extant becomes a belief-content. That of which the Being no longer can be predicated is no longer an Extant. It is the belief content, the factual and true referend, the *concretissimum,* the meontological, and not the ontological, the meontic, and not the ontic. The last link in this concept formation is the Extant become Being-toned through Being. But the meontological awareness is the fulfillment of the understanding of Being itself, and therefore the Extant as Extant cannot be the basic theme of ontology, or else a hopeless phenomenalization will take place.

Ideal Being blends neither into real Being nor into the notional representation or image. It is an intermediate stage between the two. This is to be understood from the characteristic of Being in the process of concretization. The mathematical Being of space-time, for instance, shows this character. This is why also the relationalistic-empiric theory of it is wrong in stating that space and time are relations of empirical terms and are abstracted from those. The truth is, rather, that what is seen here as the product is the producing factor, a stipulating pre-requisite of the terms, and not their subsequent relationship.

Hartmann is perfectly right in what he says about the advanced position, inobtrusiveness, unreflectedness and double disappearance of the ideal Being of mathematics, the concepts and the essences. These are valuable glimpses into the nature of ideal Being. He knows also that in doing so he merely offers similes, which are never quite accurate, and which could be improved by an investigation of the exact relationship of Being, Nothing and Extant — and this is exactly what we attempt to do here. The Extant and the thought-content, into which the abstract, ideal Being can vanish, constitute no complete disjunction. Two terms are still missing — Being and Nothing. It is of value sharply to distinguish ideal Being from these two, and to unveil the reasons of the double disappearance in the naïve awareness and in the approximation of the ideal to the notional. But this is not enough, because the disjunction is not complete, because two terms are missing which clamor for being understood in the light of their own peculiar meaning. Then, and only then, will a true understanding of transintelligibility and of the irrational and of the true essence of ideal Being be attained. To be sure, as an Extant constructed on the pattern of a thing-in-itself *(Ding an sich)*, it suffers by being approximated to the thought, and then the apperceiving awareness suffers by its narrowness. On the other hand, as Being, as contrasted with the Extant, it develops this awareness to a new breadth, and then also the simile-character of the advanced position will be justified. In the intimacy of awareness which is part and parcel of Being and Being *per se,* the strangeness to awareness now becomes an advantage. Our awareness is not equipped for ideal Being as Extant, but rather for ideal as Being. Furthermore, the irrationality and transintelligibility of the belief-content satisfies equally the requirements of Being and of the Extant as well as those of the Concrete, as to temporality, processuality, finiteness and historicality. The Ideal is the lower Being in comparison with it, but still by far not Being itself. But it is only in the belief-content that Being divests itself of the last vestige of its abstractness (which makes the Ideal the lower Being) and the synthesis with the Extant is affected. The Being-toned Extant functions here under conditions of notional representation. On the other hand, the last expression is the belief-content.

The unnatural slipping of the extant Real into a divine beyondness may be called *acosmism*. It is based on the hypostasis not only of the Extant, but also of God as an emphatically Extant. Here is the hidden error —

conceiving of God on the pattern of that-which-is-appearance. This is no place to discuss how to remedy
this. It is the ontological problem of theology. The
slipping of the Extant into Being would not be so hy-
postatical. But the theory of the belief-content supplies
the better formula of solution. Our organization is on
the way to it. So long as the goal is not reached, the
delusion will linger on — like in the case of the stick
which is held under the surface of the water appears
broken even to one who knows better.

The belief-content is also the key to the rejection of
the chorism of ideal Being. It is distinct, but not separate. It does not fuse with the Real and with Thought,
but it is no reduplication of the world. For unity rests
in the belief-content. It welds also the incomplete Being
of that which is known by Being, as such, into a unit
which cannot be dissected.

Yet, it is problematical whether the imaginary number is so devoid of all reference to reality as Hartmann
puts it. Could it not be that he, himself, lapses into a
chorism here? Just think of the use of the imaginary
number for the time dimension in the four-dimensional
space-time system of coordinates. Hartmann assumes
that there is a real space, whether Euclidian or not,
which as such has its absolute geometry. But this is
wrong. He counts his chickens before they are hatched.
He does not take in consideration the relationship to
Being and Nothing, he makes the Extant hypostatic and
absolute. In these conditions, every hope is bound to
vanish that the imaginary number and the plurality of
possible spaces may ever acquire a real meaning. But,
naturally, not all the irreal constructs are on the same
level. A sphinx has a logical possibility and a real impossibility; a "wooden iron" has both logical and real im-

possibility — but the imaginary number and the purality of spaces have a logical and a real possibility. All that is needed is to include in the latter that of Being itself, which is the Being *per se* of the Extant, and of that which is meant by the negation of Being for the all-irrational belief-content. The basis of this difference is as follows: The sphinx and the "wooden iron" are mere subjective products of imagination, but the imaginary number and non-Euclidian spaces are genuine ideal constructs of Being, of an ideal objectivity in the context of scientific material problems, under exclusion of every arbitrariness and whim of subjective fantasy.

Hartmann teaches that the Real is accidental from the point of view of the Ideal — and then he points at the greater strength of the real modalities as against the ideal modalities of essence. But as soon as the latter pass into Being itself, the ratio of strength becomes inverted. The modalities of Being gain — out of the fulfillment of the modalities of essence — a supremacy over the real modalities, in which the transcendent-realistic view, one-sided and unequilibrated, still retains the upper hand. Now then, insofar as the last step is taken to the belief-content of reality, the same process occurs once again, and this time the greater strength asserts itself with respect to the modalities of essence, real modalities, and the modalities of Being. The modalities include the following categories: Possibility and Impossibility, Factuality *(Wirklichkeit)* and Non-Factuality *(Unwirklichkeit)*, Necessity and its *two* antitheses — Accidentality and Freedom. Details must be deferred for later analyses. Hartmann devoted a book to this topic alone. That which is possible, actual, factual and necessary in the belief-content, might be impossible, non-factual and accidental in the Extant. We have already observed an approach to this state of affairs. Likewise, the freedom of the belief content might appear as necessity, but the two statements cannot be reversed. The modality and modal structure of the *concretissimum* would manifest itself as a so strongly dialectical complexity. These indications must suffice here.

The empirical triangle is always inexact as compared to the mathematical triangle, which is distinguished by an exact perfection. Hartmann is right in saying that this is because of the complexity of the Real. The Ideal must pay the price of an abstractness for its complete perfection. But in addition to this negativity, the *a priorism* of mathematic Being means something else, something positive, too. It points at the perfection of Being and beyond it at that of the *concretissimum*, which is like mathematical perfection, but without any abstractism, and it is exactly in this that it represents the fulfillment of the Extant. The imperfection of the latter is no longer an advantage in comparison with this, but a loss and a shortcoming. This is guessed and taken for granted beforehand in the case of the perfection of the mathematical. In this light, the imperfection of the Extant appears as originating in the subjective character of our relationship to it, as present in the very acceptance of the Extant as Extant, as the transcendent Extant *per se*. This subjectivity is on the march. It is a Being. Temporality, which confers upon the Extant the privilege of concreteness, is also a part of it. This shows a state of the problem that is quite different from the way Hartmann sees it.

Now we come to the discussion of Section Three. It is true that the phenomenological method of Husserl, the bracketing, the *Wesenschau*, etc., are intuitive and only make a use of the abstraction. The limitation of this method is that it remains restricted to the essentialities *(Wesenheiten)*. In this field, it does render fine service. But the dependence on subjectivity cannot be overcome this way. That requires the unfurling of the full problem of Being. Now then, if the phenomenological method still does intrude into the beyondness of intentionality, in the cases of problems of the Extant, of Being, of the Nothing, of the *concretissimum* — this is bound to lead only to inadequate results. The next step is the teaching of Husserl about the transcendental subject which falls back into the idealistic absolutization of the Extant. Phenomenological methodology must yield to the meontological one which actually leads to the goal.

The ideality of the mathematical is free, that of the essentialities *(Wesenheiten)* is bound. But in the way to Being, also this identity becomes free, until in the believed *concretissimum* Freedom itself appears in its fullness, as the great miracle and mystery. Only here do we learn to understand what freedom and independence truly mean as a category of modality. It brings along its own new evidence.

The problem of the harmony of cognition is there not only between cognition and Extant, but also between cognition and Being, the Nothing and the *concretissimum* of meontologic belief. But then also the sense of the proposition that the very possibility of delusion and error attests to the harmony which is truth itself, is strongly extended. Now there are many more possibilities to be considered than are considered by the transcendent-realistic concept of truth. And this is just the source of the enhanced possibility of explaining delusion and error. Their significance is placed on a deeper foundation, epistemologically, ontologically and meontologically.

Hartmann proceeds to speak of logical Being. This is the third ideality. (Mathematical Being and the essentialities *Wesenheiten* are the other two.) Logical Being is as free as mathematical Being, and as abstract as the essentialities. In fact, it is *the* abstract proper, the fountainhead of all abstraction. As showed by the three fundamental principles of logic, it exceeds the other two in ideal perfection, but also in tenuousness, emptiness and formalism of the abstract, for it is the abstract itself, the most general references in the structures of the intuitive mathematical and of the discursive essentialities. Yet, it is free, not bound. The truly interesting problem here is its relationship to the psychological thought process. Husserl began his remarkable career as a philosopher by liberating logic from psychologism. To be sure, he was not the first one to recognize that evil, but no one had taken such a radically active stand. Kant had distinguished himself by remarkable teachings on the relationship of logic to psychology, which he presented with great clarity — not to mention other before and after him (including also the father of logic, Aristotle). The norms of logic are no psychological laws of thought. On the contrary — real thought process violates them continually. But on the other hand, real thought process does go by them. They are its ideals, which it never attains, which it only approaches asymptotically. It is a relationship similar to that of empirical and ideal triangles.

But what does all this mean?

If we take a closer look, we find that these extreme abstractions of formal and normative logic press to concretizations which correlate logical Being and concrete Being. Thus it is a matter related to the vital logic which is not artificially isolated by the science of logic. Logic belongs in a context of concretization, which frees it from abstractness. This is the logical way into Being, into the Nothing, into the *concretissimum*. Moreover, logic bears the spotless purity of *a-priorism*, which it showed in the tenuous emptiness of its abstractness, and it introduces this purity into the fullness — and this is its epistemological, ontological and meontological function. This is how logicity performs its valuable service. The Logical is Being itself in its maximum abstractness. It is based on the old doctrine of the identity of Being and thinking, which is the nucleus of truth in this state of affairs. Because of its abstractness, logical Being stands so close to the Nothing that Hegel identified the two outright, in order to construct Becoming out of both. We cannot follow him on this path, but we can very well understand him. The *nil*-character of logical Being must not be confused with the concrete Nothing, which the concrete Being becomes with respect to the Extant, to try to be its ground and depth. This concrete Nothing means that the belief, which is the demonstration of apperception with respect to factuality, cannot even judge as to the Being of the factual and real meant here. This pleromatic *nil*-character of the great mystery does not contain the abstract logical Being, which is just a beginning, but its fulfillment. Logical Being stands at the opposite end. The fact that the psychological thought process goes by the logical Being, is part and parcel of the penetration which we have just described. This stage still shows all questionabilities of the ontology of the Extant as the Extant, and this is the source from which logical psychologism draws its dangerous energies.

But this will soon cease and be overcome. Let the movement advance farther into Being, which is the junction of so many diversities of the ontic, and farther into the Nothing and the *concretissimum*. Descriptive psychology is drafted into the service of great new tasks, and no further sacrifice need be made to psychologism.

The three normative principles of logic are the law of identity, the law of contradiction, and the law of the excluded middle. On the very last pages of his book, Hartmann speaks once again of logical Being. He shows that the three principles can subsist neither with nor without each other. Of course, this holds true for the problem situation in the realm of the Extant as Extant, which remains the definitive one for Hartmann. One cannot help admiring the objectivity and ingenuity of Hartmann in bringing this out. In fact — that which is absolutely consistent and possible in Being, in its negation and in the realm of the meontological belief-content, as fulfillment of logical Being through concretization, must appear as an extant contradiction and an existential impossibility in the realm of the Extant itself. But this is not due to a weakness of the logical, but to the weakness of the Extant as Extant, the appearance-character of which must never be overlooked. To be sure, the logical does show a weakness, but it is of another kind; it relates to the abstractness and to the purely abstract rationality. On the other hand, the weakness of the Extant is not the abstractness, but the hypostasis, the materialization, the absolutization of that-which-is-appearance, the substantialization, the unilateralization in the trancendent-realistic. And they bring along the contradiction that the logical principles cannot subsist either with or without each other. The positings with which this formal logic operates — such as *S, P,* etc. — are symbols for something extant. But what when logically there are no positings involved at all? Is it not necessary, then, to complement the incomplete disjunction based on positings, by such other terms of disjunction as Being, Nothing, Meontological and Meontic? But if the paradoxon of the "must-subsist-together" and "cannot-subsist-without-each-other" of the three principles obtains in the field of that incomplete disjunction — what happens then in the realm of the complete disjunction? Could it not be that the contradiction dissolves here and a quite different outlook presents itself? We have already shown that this is in fact the case. But it calls for a still more complete development. It is highly characteristic that in the collision of logical Being and the real world, a monstrosity appears, which originates in the realm of modality, namely, existential impossibility — and another one, originating from the realm of the logical, namely, extant contradiction — and that in the language of the Extant both together bear negative testimony to the truth which reigns in the realms of Being, of meontological and the meontic.

Mathematical Being, the essentialities (*Wesenheiten*), and the logical are still not all there is in the realm of the Ideal. The last sphere is formed by the values. They are even more detached than logical Being. They do not tell what there *is*, but what there *ought to be*. They do not go by the Real, and the Real does not go by them. This is a double independence, such as never has been met before. It denotes the difference between the Ought and the Extant. We would not say, however, as it is mostly put, "between the Ought and Being." For the Ought has a Being, too, and is, itself, a part of it. It is the ideal Being of valuability, which is part and parcel of the constitution of the Being *per se* of the Extant.

The true antithesis is that of the Ought and the Extant, and this antithesis is greater than in the case of the other Ideal, of mathematical Being, of the essentialities, and of logical Being. It is a maximum. It is the exaction, the postulate. This Ought-toned-value-state requires a purposive will in order to be realized, and the problem of freedom arises here immediately in connection with the moral question and the true relationship of the practical to the theoretical, become capable of formulation in the Kantian transition problem. Hartmann is right in basing value, as that which is to be apperceived, on feeling. He speaks of a value-sense, its value-answer and value-reaction. But the realization devolves upon the will. The value-sense is not so much an apperception of the value as a state of being affected by the value. The active factor lies in the realizing will. The value-reaction applies to something real, not to something fictional. In this connection, Hartmann speaks significantly of value-blindness, of the narrowness of value-awareness, of the difference between the historical validity of values, and the independent ideal Being of the values themselves. Once again, we must state that the critical discussion of the details must be deferred until we come to the discussion of the extensive ethics which is Hartmann's present to us.

The Being of the Ought cannot be defined more closely without a prior exact analysis of temporality in the modus of the future. For it reaches forward into the future, and backward from there. It brings out something of the Being which does not occur so in the other types of Being. The realization of the will of the value-indicating Ought sets in the process of concretization which delivers Being from its abstractness, and which is attached to it mostly in the logical, but also in the essential and the mathematical. This has led to a contrasting of Being and Ought, which in the light of concrete Being loses its justification and reveals itself rather as a categorical antithesis to the Extant. The shock of the meontological awareness leads to a reality awareness, which becomes the gushing fountain of all value-tonedness. The meontological has a purity which invests the realizing will with the power to overcome, and with a fullness which is true freedom. The theoretical and the practical are united; change of Being and change of sense are the blessed event. This is the eye-salve against value-blindness, the historical tendency of ethical development.

Neither sense not validity nor meaning nor value can be put up to oppose Being, for all these are part of Being which combines them in a concrete entity. But they have their categorical contrast to the Extant. This is something else. Beside the ethical values which have their realization in the will, there stand the esthetical, sociological and religious values, which are subject to still other laws of realization. Then, even cognition itself enters the realm of value with a retrospective effect, so that the value viewpoint represents the highest unification of the entire concrete Being which brings its categorical contrast to the All-Being in the meontological to a decision.

Now we come to the results of our critical analysis of Nicolai Hartmann. Ontology begins with a transcendent-realistic approach. Then it goes through all the transcendentalizations of transcendental idealism, eventually to end in the totally new phenomenon of the transcendental realism of meontology. The cycle closes here, and the return to the original unreflectedness has taken place. The transcendental elaborates Being in antithesis to the Extant. It ties into the lines marked by the categories of essence, essential being *(Wesen)*, essentialities *(Wesenheiten)*, thusness *(Sosein)*, the Ideal. In its developments, this Being becomes Nothing-like — in other words, it becomes that total otherwiseness of Being which appears to the Extant as non-Being, but is that which is basically meant by "Being." This is the full course of the idealistic line. The realistic line begins with the Extant as Extant, which is the ontical in antithesis to the ontological. The latter is overlaid by Being, essence, essentiality, thusness, ideality. The very influence of the transcendental, the ideal and the idealistic makes the ontical, which is the Extant, split into appearance and thing-in-itself. The last transcendentalizations bring about a merging of all motives, that leads first to the meontical, in antithesis to the ontically extant, to the ontological and to the meontological. Thus, at the conclusion of our analysis, the meontical shifts into the focus of our observation. This is where the above mentioned return to the unreflected takes place. The relationship of the meontical to the extant ontical consists in the overcoming, within the former, of the differences between appearance and thing-in-itself, as the fruit of the passage through all transcendentality, ideality and Being-likeness. Its relationship to the ontological and meontological is that in it Being has cast off the last vestiges of abstractness, and the link with the concreteness of the Extant is established. The useful function of abstractness for the ontological, for the meontological, for Being, essence and ideality, finds its limit in that which forces transcendental idealism ultimately to change into transcendental realism*. The meontical is the belief-content, the belief in which is identical with

* This is the starting point of a new "universe of discourse".

the meontological knowledge of what is basically meant by Truth and Factuality. The fact that the predication of Being and of the Extant with all appurtenances fails here, leads to the wholesome shock which has the effect of highest ontological discretion and makes the sense ready for the acceptance of all good phenomenal relationships which press toward the true Factual. This works out eschatologically for the further development of our basic structure and organization, and we are in the midst of this process of development, to elucidate the sense of which is the noble task of meontology. This most valuable theoretical awareness also discharges from itself all other values — ethical, esthetical, sociological and religious. It is the higher entity and the fountainhead of the practical and of the theoretical. That which transforms the meontical into the ontical, is the origin of all disvalue in all kinds of value, up to the problem of the evil. The harmful commingling, conversion, confusion and misconstructions exhaust the stream of purity. Hartmann's approach of ontology in the Extant as Extant is ontically bound, and therefore not free from that confusion and misconstruction. But this leads to error and delusion in the theoretical field, and to incapability of solving the personal-moral questions in the practical domain.

In the positive aspect, there is a difference between Being and the Extant, the ontological and the ontical. But in the negative aspect, the meontological non-Being is equal to the meontic non-Extant — there is no difference. The total elseness is that of both at the same time. This permits the union of the ontological transcendental-idealistic line with the ontical transcendental-realistic line in meontology. The meontical includes in itself the meontological, beforehand, for every abstractness is overcome, and the belief-content of the meonto-logically known is the *concretissimum*. This is not an inclusion of Self-Being in the Nothing. That which is included is, itself, part of this concrete Nothing. It is Nothing of Nothing — in other words, the believed *concretissimum* of the meontologic knowledge is the meontical, which possesses the highest power of denial and purification for the ontical and analyzes, criticizes and appraises it according to its approach to it. This is then the bliss and happiness of pure surrender to the inner-phenomenal relationships with their great tasks for the present and their mighty hope for the future. First, the transcendental has rationalized the irrational, then the meontological irrationalized the transcendental. But now it turns out that a thorough penetrative ration-alization and categorialization of the inner-phenomenal relationships takes place, emanating from the meontical, which is on the way to the final goal and can no more change over into *aufklärerisch* rationalism.

The argument that must be raised against Hartmann was, first, the testimony of Being against the Extant; then, however, the sense and meaning of the meontical against the ontical, the ontological and the meontolog-ical at the same time. The meontical reveals itself as the true topic of ontology*, which wants to become me-ontology. This is the plane on which a further critical debate with the three greatest modern philosophers — Nicolai Hartmann, Martin Heidegger, and Max Scheler — could prove to be fruitful.

---

* We could not begin with it, but had to pave the way to it.

INDEX

A

Abstractism, 38
Accessibility (*Zuhandensein,* Zuhandenheit), 26, 43, 112
Accidentality, 71
Acosmism, 137
Act (Akt), 24, 75
Algebra, 36
All-ness, 24
Anticipation, 82
Antinomy, 76, 96
Anxiety, 82
A posteriori, 55
A priori, 55, 98, 102, 103, 104, 108, 109, 113, 117, 134
Appearance, 11, 12, 29, 36, 60
Argumentum ad baculum, 102
Aristotle, 16, 21, 22, 24, 29, 30, 34, 41, 114, 142
Art 4

B

Being (*Sein*), xiii, 9, 10, 12, 15, 22-24, 29-35, 37-42, 44, 57, 59, 60, 61, 64, 68, 91, 93, 95, 97, 101, 106, 110, 129, 145, 148
Being a Given, 90
Being-an-Object, 76, 90
Being cannot be defined, 17
Being-content-fullness (*Seinsgehaltlichkeit*), 63
Being-for-death, 109
Being *for Me,* 90, 92
Being-full (*seinshaft*), 63
Being-ful Extant (*das seinshaft Seiende*), 60
Being fully Extant, 93
Being-in-the-World (In-der-Welt-Sein), 34

Being-likeness, 148
Being-Like-Non-Being, 9, 128, 131
Being of meaning, 17, 35
Being *per se (Ausichsein)*, 15, 28, 42, 58, 74, 75, 76, 77, 90, 92, 93, 96, 99, 102, 103, 104
Being per se *for me,* 90, 94
Being-toned, 59, 70, 99, 101, 103, 136
Being-toned Extant, 69, 91, 92, 137
Becoming, 22
Belief, 97, 110, 111, 128, 129, 143
Belief-content, 130, 131, 133, 135, 137, 139, 148, 150
Bentham, Jeremias, 12
Bonum, 21
Bergson, 87, 113
Berkeley, George, 20
Bracketing (*Einklammerung*), 19, 38

C

Care (*Besorgen*), 112
Cassirer, Ernst, 2
Causality, 54, 71, 72
Categories, 78
Certainly, 128, 130
Certainty of reality, 129
Chance, 81
Chorism, 121, 122, 138
Cognition, 86, 87, 88, 95, 99, 103, 108, 112, 113, 119, 121, 124, 147
Complete disjunction, 145
Comprehension (*Erfassen*), 76
Concern (Sorge), 85, 112
Concrete Being, 58-61, 63, 66, 67, 69-73, 90-94, 103, 108, 113, 114, 143, 147
Concrete Nothing, 111, 112, 113, 114, 128, 131, 143, 150

INDEX

INDEX

Herbert, Johann Friedrich, 94
Hereness (*Dasein*), 16, 23, 27, 45, 47, 48, 50, 51, 53, 54, 55, 61, 62, 64, 86, 110, 112
Hereness-givenness (*Daseinsgegebenheit*), 87
History, 5, 85
How, 75, 94
Husserl, Edmund, ix, 2, 7, 25, 87, 103, 122, 140, 141, 142

I

Idea, 118
Ideal (*Ideales*), 25, 123, 126
Ideal Being, 115, 116, 118, 120, 121, 126
Idealism, 37
Ideality, 65, 66, 115
Ideal possibilities, 68
Image, 119
Imaginary number, 139
Immanence, 27, 38, 60, 93, 95, 129
Indifference propositions, 38, 39, 45
Inflexibility of reality, 12
In mente, 88
Intellectus infinitus et divinus, 2, 11, 27, 43
Intentio oblqiua, 18, 19, 27, 31, 32, 33, 99, 103
Intentional object, 76, 93, 97, 98, 116, 134
Intentio recta, 18, 19, 32, 33, 74, 82, 101
Irrational, 78, 127
Irrationality, 100

J

Jaspers, Karl, ix
Jeans, 133
Judgments of hereness (*Dasein*), 47, 49
Judgments of suchness (*Sosein*), 47, 49

K

Kant, Immanuel, ix, 7, 8, 9, 31, 36, 41, 47, 48, 49, 51, 58, 59, 69, 71, 75, 94, 101, 102, 103, 117, 124, 132, 134, 135, 142
Kierkegaard, Soeren, 82, 108, 109

Knowledge (*Erkenntnis*), 7
Koehle, Eduard Joseph, xv

L

Law of identity, 127
Law of the excluded middle, 127
Leigniz, 51, 100, 126
Logic, 2, 18, 78, 100, 123, 124, 127, 143, 144
Logical, 145
Logical Being, 142

M

Marx, Karl, 5
Mathematical, 115, 116
Mathematical Being, 46, 132
Mathematical empiricism, 120
Mathematical ideality, 122
Mathematical intuitionism, 116
Mathematical subjectivism, 116
Meaning of Being, 17, 35
Meontic, 136, 145
Meontical, 148, 149, 150
Meontical fullness, 130
Meontic Non-Extant, 149
Meontological, 135, 143, 145, 148, 149, 150
Meontological awareness, 136, 147
Meontological belief-content, 144
Meontologic belief, 134, 141
Meontology, 131, 133, 147, 149, 150
Metaphysics, 29, 109
Minimum of metaphysics, 13, 14
Modalities, 41, 67, 68, 70, 139, 145
Modalities of Being (*Seinsmodalitäten*), 42
Mode (*Weise*), 25
Modus, 25
Mode of Being (*Seinsweise*), 24, 42, 55
Modes of givenness (Gegebenheitsweisen), 55
Modus of life, 84
Monad, 24

N

Natorp, Paul, 2

153

INDEX

154

INDEX